EVERYDAY Literacy
Reading & Writing

GRADE
1

Download Parent Letters in Spanish

Each week, there is a Home–School Connection Letter to send home with students. These letters are available in Spanish on our website.

How to Download:

1. Go to www.evan-moor.com/resources.

2. Enter your e-mail address and the resource code for this product—EMC2419.

3. You will receive an e-mail with a link to the downloadable letters, as well as an attachment with instructions.

Writing: Barbara Allman
Content Editing: Lisa Vitarisi Mathews
Joy Evans
Copy Editing: Cathy Harber
Art Direction: Cheryl Puckett
Kathy Kopp
Cover Design: Cheryl Puckett
Cover Illustration: Shirley Beckes
Illustration: Ann Iosa
Design/Production: Carolina Caird
Yuki Meyer

EMC 2419

Evan-Moor
EDUCATIONAL PUBLISHERS®
Helping Children Learn since 1979

Congratulations on your purchase of some of the finest teaching materials in the world.

For information about other Evan-Moor products, call 1-800-777-4362, fax 1-800-777-4332, or visit our Web site, www.evan-moor.com. Entire contents © 2011 EVAN-MOOR CORP. 18 Lower Ragsdale Drive, Monterey, CA 93940-5746. Printed in USA.

Correlated
to State Standards

Visit *teaching-standards.com* to view a correlation of this book's activities to your state's standards. This is a free service.

CPSIA: QuadGraphics Dubuque, 2470 Kerper Boulevard, Dubuque, IA USA. 52001 [12/2010]

Contents

What's Inside?

In this book, you will find **20 weekly lessons**. Each weekly lesson includes:

3 Teacher Pages

Use these pages to guide you through the week.

A script to follow that introduces the word family.

A short story to read aloud to students

Daily discussion questions about the story, plus a script to guide students through the activities

An oral language activity that reviews the week's families.

A sample of students' expected response

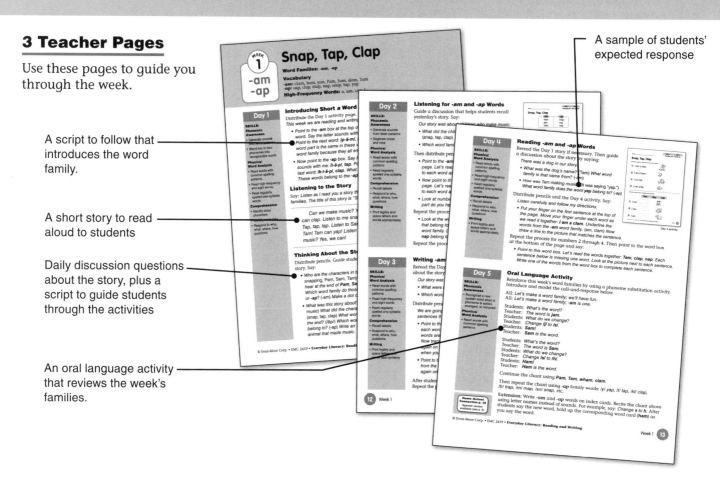

4 Student Activity Pages

Reproduce each page for students to complete during the daily lesson.

1 Home–School Connection Page

At the end of each week, give students the **Home–School Connection** page (in English or Spanish) to take home and share with their parents.

To access the Spanish version of the activity, go to www.evan-moor.com/resources. Enter your e-mail address and the resource code EMC2419.

Note to parents

How to Use This Book

Follow these easy steps to conduct the lessons:

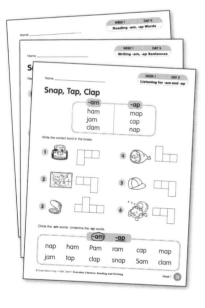

Home–School Connection

Day 1

Reproduce and distribute the *Day 1 Student Page* to each child.

Using the scripted *Day 1 Teacher Page:*

1. Introduce the week's word families.

2. Read the story aloud as students listen and look at the picture.

3. Guide students through the activity.

Days 2, 3, 4

Reproduce and distribute the appropriate day's activity page to each student.

Using the scripted *Teacher Page:*

1. Review and discuss the Day 1 story.

2. Introduce and model the skill or concept.

3. Guide students through the activity.

Day 5

Follow the directions to lead students through the Oral Language Activity.

Send home the **Home–School Connection** page with each student to complete with his or her parents.

Tips for Success

- Review the *Teacher Page* before you begin the lesson.

- Wait for students to complete each task before giving the next direction.

- Model how to respond to questions by using complete sentences. For example, if a student responds to the question "Who does the dog belong to?" by answering "the girl," you'd respond, "That's right. The dog belongs to the girl."

- Model how to orally blend three-letter words emphasizing onset and rime. For example, /t...ub/.

- Encourage students to say words aloud. Model correct pronunciation when necessary.

- Make a word wall that displays each week's word families.

- Dictate the week's word family words to students and have them write each word. After you finish dictating the words, have students draw a picture beside each word to show what it means.

Dear Parent or Guardian,

Every week your child will complete reading and writing activities that focus on word families, words that have the same ending sounds. For example, *tan, fan, pan, ran*. The activities provide a fun and easy way for your child to increase his or her reading and writing vocabulary.

At the end of each week, I will send home an activity page for you to complete with your child. The activity page includes a reading activity and a writing activity for you and your child to do together.

Sincerely,

Estimado padre o tutor:

Cada semana su niño(a) completará actividades de lecto-escritura enfocadas sobre familias de palabras. Las familias de palabras terminan con el mismo sonido, como por ejemplo *tan, fan, pan, ran*. Estas actividades, además de divertidas, ayudan a su niño(a) a ampliar su vocabulario de lecto-escritura.

Al final de cada semana, le enviaré una hoja que explica las actividades que puede realizar con su niño(a). La hoja contiene una actividad de lectura y una actividad de escritura que pueden hacer juntos en casa.

Sinceramente,

Everyday Literacy: Reading and Writing • EMC 2419 • © Evan-Moor Corp.

Skills Chart

Week	Generate sounds from letter patterns	Blend two to four phonemes into recognizable words	Segment onset and rime	Recognize a new spoken word when a phoneme is added, changed, or removed	Read words with common spelling patterns	Read high-frequency and sight words	Read regularly spelled one-syllable words	Identify story characters	Identify main idea	Respond to who, what, where, how questions	Recall details	Describe a picture using complete sentences	Use context clues to decode words	Print legibly and space letters and words appropriately	Use developing knowledge of letter-sound correspondences to spell independently
Phonemic Awareness					**Phonics/Word Analysis**			**Comprehension**						**Writing**	
1	•	•	•	•	•	•	•	•	•	•	•			•	
2	•	•	•	•	•	•	•	•	•	•				•	
3	•	•			•	•	•					•	•	•	•
4	•	•	•	•	•	•	•	•	•	•	•			•	
5	•	•	•	•	•	•	•	•	•	•	•			•	
6	•	•			•	•	•					•	•	•	•
7	•	•	•	•	•	•	•	•	•	•	•			•	
8	•	•	•	•	•	•	•	•	•	•	•			•	
9	•	•			•	•	•					•	•	•	•
10	•	•	•	•	•	•	•	•	•	•	•			•	
11	•	•	•	•	•	•	•	•	•	•	•			•	
12	•	•			•	•	•					•	•	•	•
13	•	•	•	•	•	•	•	•	•	•	•			•	
14	•	•	•	•	•	•	•	•	•	•	•			•	
15	•	•			•	•	•					•	•	•	•
16	•	•	•	•	•	•	•	•	•	•	•			•	
17	•	•	•	•	•	•	•	•	•	•	•			•	
18	•	•	•	•	•	•	•	•	•	•	•			•	
19	•	•	•	•	•	•	•	•	•	•	•			•	
20	•	•	•	•	•	•	•	•	•	•	•			•	

Everyday Literacy
Reading and Writing

Student Progress Record

Name: _____

Write dates and comments below the student's proficiency level.

1: Rarely demonstrates   0 – 25 %
2: Occasionally demonstrates   25 – 50 %
3: Usually demonstrates   50 – 75 %
4: Consistently demonstrates   75 – 100 %

Phonemic Awareness

	1	2	3	4
Generates sounds from letter patterns				
Blends two to four phonemes into recognizable words				
Segments onset and rime				
Recognizes a new spoken word when a phoneme is added, changed, or removed				

Phonics/Word Analysis

Reads words with common spelling patterns				
Reads high-frequency and sight words				
Reads regularly spelled one-syllable words				

Comprehension

Identifies story characters				
Responds to *who, what, where, how* questions				
Describes a picture using complete sentences				
Uses context clues to decode words				

Writing

Prints legibly and spaces letters and words appropriately				
Uses developing knowledge of letter-sound correspondences to spell independently				

Everyday Literacy
Reading and Writing

Small Group Record Sheet

Students' Names:

Write dates and comments about students' performance each week.

Week	Title	Comments
1	Snap, Tap, Clap—*am, ap*	
2	Stan the Cat—*an, at*	
3	Review It —*short a words*	
4	Will a Hen Get Wet?—*en, et*	
5	Nell and the Red Sled—*ell, ed*	
6	Review It—*short e words*	
7	Can Miss Pig Win?—*ig, in*	
8	Let's Knit—*ip, it*	
9	Review It—*short i words*	
10	Bob's Shop—*ob, op*	
11	Dog Meets Frog—*og, ot*	
12	Review It—*short o words*	
13	Fun in a Tub—*ub, ug*	
14	Out Goes the Junk—*um, unk*	
15	Review It —*short u words*	
16	Slide, Glide, Ride on Ice—*ice, ide*	
17	Snow Day—*old, ow*	
18	Dune Lake—*ue, une*	
19	At the Beach—*each, ear*	
20	A Skate Party—*ake, ate*	

Snap, Tap, Clap

Word Families: *-am, -ap*

Vocabulary
-am: clam, ham, jam, Pam, Sam, slam, Tam
-ap: cap, clap, map, nap, snap, tap, yap

High-Frequency Words: a, am, can, I

Day 1

SKILLS:

Phonemic Awareness
- Generate sounds from letter patterns
- Blend two to four phonemes into recognizable words

Phonics/ Word Analysis
- Read words with common spelling patterns
- Read high-frequency and sight words
- Read regularly spelled one-syllable words

Comprehension
- Identify story characters
- Identify main idea
- Respond to who, what, where, how questions

Introducing Short *a* Word Families: *-am, -ap*

Distribute the Day 1 activity page. Point to each word ending as you say: *This week we are reading and writing two short **a** word families: /ăm/ and /ăp/.*

- *Point to the **-am** box at the top of the page. Say /ăm/. (/ăm/) Point to the first word. Say the letter sounds with me: /s-ă-m/. Blend the sounds together: **Sam**. Point to the next word: /p-ă-m/, **Pam**. Point to the last word: /t-ă-m/, **Tam**. What word part is the same in these words? (/ăm/) These words belong to the **-am** word family because they all end with **am**.*

- *Now point to the **-ap** box. Say /ăp/. (/ăp/) Point to the first word. Say the letter sounds with me: /t-ă-p/, **tap**. Point to the next word: /y-ă-p/, **yap**. Point to the last word: /k-l-ă-p/, **clap**. What word part is the same in these words? (/ăp/) These words belong to the **-ap** word family because they all end with **ap**.*

Listening to the Story

Say: *Listen as I read you a story that has words from the **-am** and the **-ap** word families. The title of this story is "Snap, Tap, Clap."*

Can we make music? Yes, we can! I can snap. Pam can tap. Sam can clap. Listen to me snap. Snap, snap, snap. Listen to Pam tap. Tap, tap, tap. Listen to Sam clap. Clap, clap, clap. Oh, I almost forgot Tam! Tam can yap! Listen to Tam yap. Yap, yap, yap! Can we make music? Yes, we can!

Thinking About the Story

Distribute pencils. Guide students in discussing the story. Say:

- *Who are the characters in this story?* (the girl snapping, Pam, Sam, Tam) *What word part do you hear at the end of **Pam, Sam,** and **Tam**?* (/ăm/) *Which word family do those names belong to: **-am** or **-ap**?* (-am) *Make a dot on **Pam, Sam,** and **Tam**.*

- *What was this story about?* (children making music) *What did the characters do to make music?* (snap, tap, clap) *What word part do you hear at the end?* (/ăp/) *Which word family do those words belong to?* (-ap) *Write an **X** on each person or animal that made music.*

Day 1 picture

Day 2

SKILLS:

Phonemic Awareness

- Generate sounds from letter patterns
- Segment onset and rime

Phonics/ Word Analysis

- Read words with common spelling patterns
- Read regularly spelled one-syllable words

Comprehension

- Recall details
- Respond to who, what, where, how questions

Writing

- Print legibly and space letters and words appropriately

Listening for *-am* and *-ap* Words

Guide a discussion that helps students recall yesterday's story. Say:

Our story was about children who make music.

- *What did the children do to make music?* (snap, tap, clap)

- *Which word family do those words belong to?* (-ap)

Then distribute pencils and the Day 2 activity. Say:

- *Point to the* **-am** *word family at the top of the page. Let's read the* **-am** *words together. Point to each word as we read:* **ham, jam, clam.**

- *Now point to the* **-ap** *word family at the top of the page. Let's read the* **-ap** *words together. Point to each word as we read:* **map, cap, nap.**

- *Look at number 1. It shows jam. What is the first sound in* **jam**? (/j/) *Which word part do you hear at the* <u>end</u> *of* **jam**? (/ăm/) *Write the word* **jam** *in the boxes.*

Repeat the process for numbers 2 through 6. Then say:

- *Look at the words at the bottom of the page. Read each word. Circle the words that belong to the* **-am** *word family. Underline the words that belong to the* **-ap** *word family. Let's read the first word together:* **nap.** *Which word family does* **nap** *belong to?* (-ap) *Draw a line under* **nap.**

Repeat the process for the remaining words.

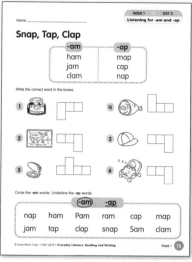

Day 2 activity

Day 3

SKILLS:

Phonics/ Word Analysis

- Read words with common spelling patterns
- Read high-frequency and sight words
- Read regularly spelled one-syllable words

Comprehension

- Recall details
- Respond to who, what, where, how questions

Writing

- Print legibly and space letters and words appropriately

Writing *-am* and *-ap* Sentences

Reread the Day 1 story. Then guide a discussion about the story by saying:

Our story was about children who snap, tap, and clap.

- *What were the children's names?* (Sam and Pam)

- *Which word family do their names belong to?* (-am)

Distribute pencils and the Day 3 activity. Say:

We are going to read, trace, and then write sentences that have **-am** *and* **-ap** *words.*

- *Point to the first sentence. Move your finger under each word as we read together:* **I am Pam.** *Which words are from the* **-am** *word family?* (am, Pam) *Now trace the sentence, then write the sentence again on the line below. Put your pencil down when you are finished.*

- *Point to the next sentence. Let's read it together:* **I can tap.** *Which word is from the* **-ap** *word family?* (tap) *Trace the sentence, then write the sentence again on the line below. Put your pencil down when you are finished.*

Day 3 activity

After students complete sentence 2, have them read sentences 1 and 2 aloud. Repeat the process for sentences 3 and 4.

Everyday Literacy: Reading and Writing • EMC 2419 • © Evan-Moor Corp.

SKILLS:

**Phonics/
Word Analysis**

- Read words with common spelling patterns
- Read high-frequency and sight words
- Read regularly spelled one-syllable words

Comprehension

- Recall details
- Respond to who, what, where, how questions

Writing

- Print legibly and space letters and words appropriately

Reading *-am* and *-ap* Words

Reread the Day 1 story if necessary. Then guide a discussion about the story by saying:

There was a dog in our story.

- *What was the dog's name? (Tam) What word family is that name from? (-am)*

- *How was Tam making music? (It was saying "yap.") What word family does the word **yap** belong to? (-ap)*

Distribute pencils and the Day 4 activity. Say:

Listen carefully and follow my directions.

- *Put your finger on the first sentence at the top of the page. Move your finger under each word as we read it together: **I am a clam.** Underline the words from the **-am** word family. (am, clam) Now draw a line to the picture that matches the sentence.*

Repeat the process for numbers 2 through 4. Then point to the word box at the bottom of the page and say:

- *Point to this word box. Let's read the words together: **Tam, clap, nap.** Each sentence below is missing one word. Look at the picture next to each sentence. Write one of the words from the word box to complete each sentence.*

Day 4 activity

Oral Language Activity

Reinforce this week's word families by using a phoneme substitution activity. Introduce and model the call-and-response below.

All: *Let's make a word family; we'll have fun.*
All: *Let's make a word family; **-am** is one.*

Students: *What's the word?*
Teacher: *The word is **jam.***
Students: *What do we change?*
Teacher: *Change /j/ to /s/.*
Students: ***Sam!***
Teacher: ***Sam** is the word.*

Students: *What's the word?*
Teacher: *The word is **Sam.***
Students: *What do we change?*
Teacher: *Change /s/ to /h/.*
Students: ***Ham!***
Teacher: ***Ham** is the word.*

Continue the chant using **Pam, Tam, wham, clam.**

Then repeat the chant using **-ap** family words: */y/ yap, /t/ tap, /kl/ clap, /tr/ trap, /m/ map, /sn/ snap,* etc.

Extension: Write **-am** and **-ap** words on index cards. Recite the chant above using letter names instead of sounds. For example, say: *Change **s** to **h**.* After students say the new word, hold up the corresponding word card (**ham**) as you say the word.

Day 5

SKILLS:

**Phonemic
Awareness**

- Recognize a new spoken word when a phoneme is added, changed, or removed

**Phonics/
Word Analysis**

- Read words with common spelling patterns

**Home–School
Connection p. 18**
Spanish version available (see p. 2)

Snap, Tap, Clap

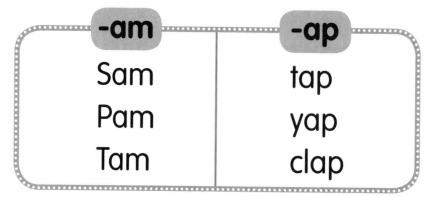

-am	-ap	
Sam	tap	
Pam	yap	
Tam	clap	

Name _____

Snap, Tap, Clap

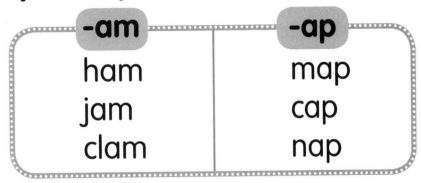

-am	-ap
ham	map
jam	cap
clam	nap

Write the correct word in the boxes.

 1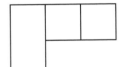

2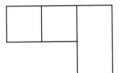

3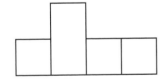

4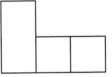

5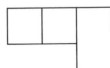

6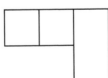

Circle the **-am** words. Underline the **-ap** words.

(-am)   -ap

nap   ham   Pam   ram   cap   map

jam   tap   clap   snap   Sam   clam

Snap, Tap, Clap

Read the sentence. Trace the sentence. Then write the sentence on the line below.

1 I am Pam.

2 I can tap.

3 I am Sam.

4 I can clap.

Everyday Literacy: Reading and Writing • EMC 2419 • © Evan-Moor Corp.

Name _____

Snap, Tap, Clap

Read the sentence. Draw a line to the correct picture.

1 I am a clam.

2 I am a ham.

3 I can tap.

4 I can snap.

Write the correct word to complete each sentence.

Tam   clap   nap

1 I can _____.

2 I can _____.

3 I am _____.

Name _____

Snap, Tap, Clap

What to Do
Read the story with your child and look at the picture together.
Then have your child circle words in the story that end with **-am**
and draw a line under words that end with **-ap**.

WEEK 1

Home–School Connection

To Parents
This week your child learned to read and write words from the **-am** and **-ap** word families.

I can snap. Snap, snap, snap! Pam can tap.
Tap, tap, tap! Sam can clap. Clap, clap, clap!
Tam can yap. Yap, yap, yap!

What to Do Next
Work together with your child to write a story using words from the **-am** and **-ap** word families.

Everyday Literacy: Reading and Writing • EMC 2419 • © Evan-Moor Corp.

Stan the Cat

Word Families
-an, -at
Vocabulary
-an: fan, man, pan, plan, ran, Stan, tan, van
-at: bat, cat, hat, mat, rat, sat, scat, that
High-Frequency Words: a, can, go, I, is, it, made, on, said, see, the

Day 1

SKILLS:
Phonemic Awareness
• Generate sounds from letter patterns
• Blend two to four phonemes into recognizable words

Phonics/ Word Analysis
• Read words with common spelling patterns
• Read high-frequency and sight words
• Read regularly spelled one-syllable words

Comprehension
• Identify story characters
• Identify main idea
• Respond to who, what, where, how questions

Introducing Short *a* Word Families: *-an, -at*

Distribute the Day 1 activity page. Say: *This week we are reading and writing two more short **a** word families: **/ăn/** and **/ăt/**.*

- *Point to the **-an** box at the top of the page. Say **/ăn/**. (/ăn/) Point to the first word. Say the letter sounds with me: **/f-ă-n/**. Blend the sounds together: **fan**. Point to the next word: **/p-ă-n/, pan**. Point to the last word: **/m-ă-n/, man**. What word part is the same in all of these words? (/ăn/) These words belong to the **-an** word family.*

- *Now point to the **-at** box. Say **/ăt/**. (/ăt/) Point to the first word. Say the letter sounds with me: **/k-ă-t/, cat**. Point to the next word: **/h-ă-t/, hat**. Point to the last word: **/m-ă-t/, mat**. What word part is the same in all of these words? (/ăt/) These words belong to the **-at** word family.*

Listening to the Story

Say: *Listen as I read you a story that has words from the **-an** and the **-at** word families. The title of this story is "Stan the Cat."*

Stan is my tan cat. Stan likes to sit on the mat. He watches while Mom cooks. One day, he sat on the mat. He was in Mom's way. Mom wanted Stan to move. She had a pan. She said, "Scat, cat!" But Stan sat and sat. Mom turned on the cooking fan. That cat ran! I guess Stan did not like the fan.

Thinking About the Story

Distribute pencils. Guide students in discussing the story. Say:

- *Where does the cat in this story sit?* (on a mat) *What word part do you hear at the end of **cat** and **mat**?* (/ăt/) *Which word family do those words belong to: **-an** or **-at**?* (-at) *Make a dot on the **cat** and on the **mat**.*

- *What was the cat's name?* (Stan) *What did Stan do at the end of the story?* (ran) *What made Stan run?* (fan) *What word part do you hear at the end of **ran**, **Stan**, and **fan**?* (/ăn/) *Which word family do those words belong to?* (-an) *Write an **X** beside **Stan**.*

Day 1 picture

SKILLS:

Phonemic Awareness

• Generate sounds from letter patterns

• Segment onset and rime

Phonics/ Word Analysis

• Read words with common spelling patterns

• Read high-frequency and sight words

• Read regularly spelled one-syllable words

Comprehension

• Recall details

• Respond to who, what, where, how questions

Writing

• Print legibly and space letters and words appropriately

Listening for *-an* and *-at* Words

Guide a discussion that helps students recall yesterday's story. Say:

Our story was about Stan the cat. What did Stan dislike? (the fan) What did he do when the fan was turned on? (he ran)

• *Which word family do the words **fan**, **ran**, and **Stan** belong to? (-an)*

Then distribute pencils and the Day 2 activity. Say:

• *Point to the **-an** word family at the top of the page. Let's read the **-an** words together. Point to each word as we read: **man**, **pan**, **van**.*

• *Now point to the **-at** word family at the top of the page. Let's read the **-at** words together. Point to each word as we read: **bat**, **hat**, **rat**.*

• *Look at number 1. It shows a van. What is the first sound in **van**? (/v/) Which word part do you hear at the end of **van**? (/ăn/) Write the word **van** in the boxes.*

Repeat the process for numbers 2 through 6. Then say:

• *Look at the words at the bottom of the page. Read each word. Circle the words that belong to the **-an** word family. Underline the words that belong to the **-at** word family. Let's read the first word together: **tan**. Which word family does **tan** belong to? (-an) Circle the word **tan**.*

Repeat the process for the remaining words.

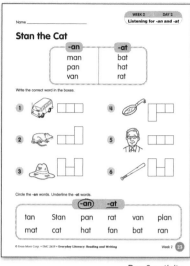

Day 2 activity

SKILLS:

Phonics/ Word Analysis

• Read words with common spelling patterns

• Read high-frequency and sight words

• Read regularly spelled one-syllable words

Comprehension

• Recall details

• Respond to who, what, where, how questions

Writing

• Print legibly and space letters and words appropriately

Writing *-an* and *-at* Sentences

Reread the Day 1 story. Then guide a discussion about the story by saying:

Our story was about a cat that ran off a mat. What did Mom say to the cat? ("Scat, cat!")

• *Which word family do the words **mat** and **scat** belong to? (-at)*

Distribute pencils and the Day 3 activity. Say:

*We are going to read, trace, and then write sentences that have **-an** and **-at** words.*

• *Point to the first sentence. Move your finger under each word as we read together: **The cat sat**. Which words are from the **-at** word family? (cat, sat) Now trace the sentence, then write the sentence again on the line below. Put your pencil down when you are finished.*

• *Point to the next sentence. Let's read it together: **It sat on a mat**. Which words are from the **-at** word family? (sat, mat) Trace the sentence, then write the sentence again on the line below. Put your pencil down when you are finished.*

After students complete sentence 2, have them read sentences 1 and 2 aloud. Repeat the process for sentences 3 and 4.

Day 3 activity

Day 4

SKILLS:

**Phonics/
Word Analysis**
- Read words with common spelling patterns
- Read high-frequency and sight words
- Read regularly spelled one-syllable words

Comprehension
- Recall details
- Respond to who, what, where, how questions

Writing
- Print legibly and space letters and words appropriately

Reading *-an* and *-at* Words

Reread the Day 1 story if necessary. Then guide a discussion about the story by saying:

There was a cat in our story. What was the cat's name? (Stan) *What word family does the name **Stan** belong to?* (-an)

- *Where did Stan sit?* (on a mat) *What word family does the word **mat** belong to?* (-at)

Distribute pencils and the Day 4 activity. Say:

Listen carefully and follow my directions.

- *Put your finger on the first sentence at the top of the page. Move your finger under each word as we read it together: **I can fan.** Underline the words from the **-an** word family. (can, fan) Draw a line to the picture that matches the sentence.*

Repeat the process for numbers 2 through 4. Then point to the word box at the bottom of the page and say:

- *Point to this word box. Let's read the words together: **bat**, **hat**, **man**. Each sentence below is missing one word. Look at the picture next to each sentence. Write one of the words from the word box to complete each sentence.*

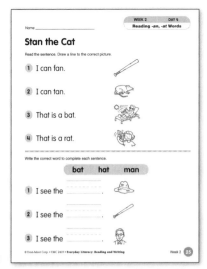

Day 4 activity

Day 5

SKILLS:

Phonemic Awareness
- Recognize a new spoken word when a phoneme is added, changed, or removed

**Phonics/
Word Analysis**
- Read words with common spelling patterns

Oral Language Activity

Reinforce this week's word families by using a phoneme substitution activity. Introduce and model the call-and-response below.

All: *Let's make a word family; we'll have fun.*
All: *Let's make a word family; **-an** is one.*

Students: *What's the word?*
Teacher: *The word is **ran**.*
Students: *What do we change?*
Teacher: *Change /r/ to /p/.*
Students: ***Pan!***
Teacher: ***Pan** is the word.*

Students: *What's the word?*
Teacher: *The word is **pan**.*
Students: *What do we change?*
Teacher: *Change /p/ to /k/.*
Students: ***Can!***
Teacher: ***Can** is the word.*

Continue the chant using **man**, **tan**, **plan**, **fan**.

Then repeat the chant using **-at** family words: /s/ *sat*, /p/ *pat*, /r/ *rat*, /f/ *fat*, /m/ *mat*, /k/ *cat*, etc.

Extension: Write **-an** and **-at** words on index cards. Recite the chant above using letter names instead of sounds. For example, say: *Change **p** to **c**.* After students say the new word, hold up the corresponding word card (**can**) as you say the word.

**Home–School
Connection p. 26**
Spanish version available (see p. 2)

Name _____

Stan the Cat

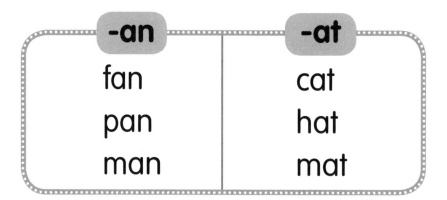

-an	-at
fan	cat
pan	hat
man	mat

Name _____

Stan the Cat

-an	-at
man	bat
pan	hat
van	rat

Write the correct word in the boxes.

1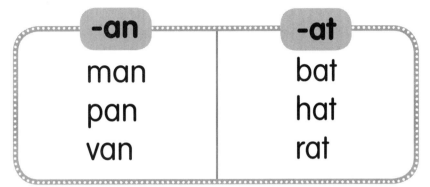

2

3

4

5

6

Circle the **-an** words. Underline the **-at** words.

(-an)   -at

tan	Stan	pan	rat	van	plan
mat	cat	hat	fan	bat	ran

Name _____

Stan the Cat

Read the sentence. Trace the sentence. Then write the sentence on the line below.

1 The cat sat.

2 It sat on a mat.

3 See the fan.

4 The cat ran.

Everyday Literacy: Reading and Writing • EMC 2419 • © Evan-Moor Corp.

Name _____

Stan the Cat

Read the sentence. Draw a line to the correct picture.

1 I can fan.

2 I can tan.

3 That is a bat.

4 That is a rat.

Write the correct word to complete each sentence.

bat   hat   man

1 I see the _____ .

2 I see the _____ .

3 I see the _____ .

Name _____

Stan the Cat

What to Do
Read the story with your child and look at the picture together.
Then have your child circle words in the story that end with **-an**
and draw a line under words that end with **-at**.

Stan is a tan cat. Stan sat on the mat.
Mom said, "Scat, cat!" Stan sat and sat.
Mom made the fan go. That cat ran!

What to Do Next
Work together with your child to write a story using words from the **-an** and **-at** word families.

Review It

Short *a* Word Family Words:
-am: clam, ham, jam, Pam, Sam, slam
-ap: cap, clap, map, nap, tap
-an: bran, can, fan, man, pan, ran, Stan
-at: bat, cat, flat, hat, rat, sat, scat

High-Frequency Words: a, am, big, can, from, I, is, it, see, that, the, this

Day 1

SKILLS:
Phonemic Awareness
• Generate sounds from letter patterns
• Blend two to four phonemes into recognizable words

Phonics/Word Analysis
• Read words with common spelling patterns
• Read regularly spelled one-syllable words

Listening for Short *a* Word Families

Distribute the Day 1 activity and a pencil to each student. Then say:

• *Let's review the short **a** word families we learned during the past few weeks. Point to each gray box as we read each word family ending together: **-ap**, **-an**, **-at**, **-am**. Now we'll match each picture to its word family. Point to the cap. Say **cap**. (cap) What word family does **cap** belong to? (-ap) What letters stand for /ăp/? (ap) Draw a line from the cap to the correct word family.*

• *Point to Sam. Say **Sam**. (Sam) What word family does **Sam** belong to? (-am) What letters stand for /ăm/? (am) Draw a line from Sam to the correct word family.*

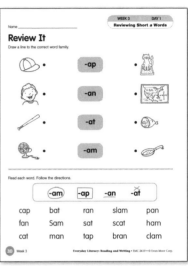

Day 1 activity

• *Point to the bat. Say **bat**. (bat) What word family does **bat** belong to? (-at) What letters stand for /ăt/? (at) Draw a line from the bat to the correct word family.*

Repeat the process for the remaining picture words: **fan, cat, map, ham,** and **pan**.

Discriminating *-am, -ap, -an, -at*

Direct students' attention to the bottom half of the page. Say:

• *These words belong to short **a** word families. We're going to read each word and follow the directions shown in the box. Let's start with the **-am** word family. When you read a word that belongs to the **-am** family, draw a circle around it. Do that now. (pause) Which words did you circle? (Sam, slam, ham, clam)*

• *Now look for words from the **-ap** word family. When you read a word that belongs to the **-ap** family, draw a box around it. Do that now. (pause) Which words did you box? (cap, tap)*

• *Now look for words from the **-an** word family. When you read a word that belongs to the **-an** family, draw a line under it. Do that now. (pause) Which words did you underline? (fan, man, ran, bran, pan)*

• *Now look for words from the **-at** word family. When you read a word that belongs to the **-at** family, write an **X** above it. Do that now. (pause) Which words did you mark with an **X**? (cat, bat, sat, scat)*

Day 2

SKILLS:

Phonemic Awareness
• Segment onset and rime

Phonics/ Word Analysis
• Read words with common spelling patterns
• Read high-frequency and sight words
• Read regularly spelled one-syllable words

Writing
• Print legibly and space letters and words appropriately

Writing Short *a* Word Family Words

Distribute the Day 2 activity and a pencil to each student. Then say:

• *Look at the word endings in the box. Let's read them together: **-am, -ap, -an, -at**. Now look at the pictures below.*

• *Point to picture number 1. It shows a can. Which word family does **can** belong to? (-an) Write the missing letters to finish the word **can**.*

• *Point to picture number 2. It shows a cat. Which word family does **cat** belong to? (-at) Write the missing letters to finish the word **cat**.*

Repeat the process for the remaining words: **Sam, sat, map, man, clap, clam**. Then say:

• *Now we're going to read sentences and draw a line to the matching picture. Point to number 1. Let's read together: **I am Sam. I can clap.** Draw a line to the picture that matches.*

Repeat the process for the remaining sentences.

Day 2 activity

Day 3

SKILLS:

Phonics/ Word Analysis
• Read words with common spelling patterns
• Read high-frequency and sight words
• Read regularly spelled one-syllable words

Writing
• Use developing knowledge of letter-sound correspondences to spell independently
• Print legibly and space letters and words appropriately

Reading *-am, -ap, -an, -at*

Distribute the Day 3 activity and a pencil to each student. Say:

• *The words in the box belong to short **a** word families. Point to each word and read with me: **ham, cat, jam, fan, pan, mat, clap, rat, clam, map**.*

• *Point to sentence number 1. Move your finger under each word as we read together: **The (blank) sat**. What does the picture show? (cat) Write **cat** to complete the sentence. Use the word box if you need help.*

• *Read sentence 2: **I see the (blank)**. What does the picture show? (map) Write **map** in the sentence.*

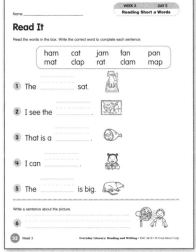

Day 3 activity

• *Read sentence 3: **That is a (blank)**. What does the picture show? (ham) Write **ham** in the sentence.*

• *Read sentence 4: **I can (blank)**. What does the picture show? (clap) Write **clap** in the sentence.*

• *Read sentence 5: **The (blank) is big**. What does the picture show? (rat) Write **rat** in the sentence.*

• *Now let's read all of the sentences together. Move your finger under each word as we read. Number 1: **The cat sat**. 2. **I see the map**. 3. **That is a ham**. 4. **I can clap**. 5. **The rat is big**.*

• *Point to number 6. What do you see in the picture? (A boy is cooling off in front of a fan.) Write a sentence about the picture. (Answers vary.) Then read your sentence to a classmate.*

<table>
<tr><td>

Day 4

SKILLS:
Phonics/
Word Analysis
- Read words with common spelling patterns
- Read high-frequency and sight words
- Read regularly spelled one-syllable words

Comprehension
- Describe a picture using complete sentences

Writing
- Use developing knowledge of letter-sound correspondences to spell independently
- Print legibly and space letters and words appropriately

</td></tr>
</table>

Writing Short *a* Word Sentences

Distribute the Day 4 activity and a pencil to each student. Then say:

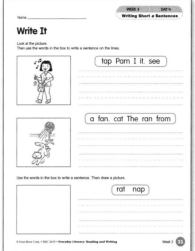

Day 4 activity

- *Look at the first picture. What do you see?* (a girl tapping a drum) *Now look at the words in the first box. These words make up a sentence that tells about the picture. The words are out of order. Unscramble the words to write a sentence about the picture. Put your pencil down when you are finished.*

- *Look at the next picture. What do you see?* (a cat running from a fan) *Now look at the words in the box. These words make up a sentence that tells about the picture. The words are out of order. Unscramble the words to write a sentence about the picture. Put your pencil down when you are finished.*

- *Look at the words in the last box. Point to each word as we read it:* **rat**, **nap**. *Write a sentence that uses these words. Then draw a picture about your sentence.* (Answers vary.)

Day 5

SKILLS:
Phonics/
Word Analysis
- Read words with common spelling patterns

Comprehension
- Use context clues to decode words

Phonics Game

Review the short **a** word families students learned this week by playing the following game.

Materials: 4 index cards per group, labeled -**am**, -**ap**, -**an**, and -**at**

Preparation: Divide the class into groups of four. Give each group a set of word family cards.

How to Play: Pick a "mystery word" from the chart below and write its first letter (or blend) on the board. Have students in each group sort through their word family cards and find all the cards that can be added to that letter to form a word. For example, if you write **p** on the board, students should determine that they can form **Pam**, **pan**, and **pat**.

Then give students the mystery word's clue from the chart, and have each group decide what the mystery word is (e.g., "something you cook with" must be "pan") and the word family card that can be used to form it (-**an**). Ask a volunteer from each group to hold up the correct card.

Home–School
Connection p. 34
Spanish version available (see p. 2)

Mystery Word	Clue	Mystery Word	Clue
pan	something you cook with	**hat**	something you wear
sat	stayed in a chair	**ran**	went fast
man	a grown-up boy	**flat**	like a pancake
tap	a type of dance with special shoes	**clap**	what you do with your hands

Review It

Draw a line to the correct word family.

 •

-ap

•

 •

-an

•

 •

-at

•

 •

-am

•

Read each word. Follow the directions.

(-am)	-ap	-an	✗ -at

cap	bat	ran	slam	pan
fan	Sam	sat	scat	ham
cat	man	tap	bran	clam

Everyday Literacy: Reading and Writing • EMC 2419 • © Evan-Moor Corp.

Name _____

Write It

Which word family do you hear?
Write **am**, **ap**, **an**, or **at** to spell each word.

-am   -ap   -an   -at

1 c _____

2 c _____

3 S _____

4 S _____

5  m _____

6 m _____

7 cl _____

8 cl _____

Read the sentences. Draw a line to the correct picture.

1 I am Sam.

I can clap.

•

2 This is Stan.

Stan is a cat.

•

Name _____

Read It

Read the words in the box. Write the correct word to complete each sentence.

ham	cat	jam	fan	pan
mat	clap	rat	clam	map

1 The _____ sat.

2 I see the _____ .

3 That is a _____ .

4 I can _____ .

5 The _____ is big.

Write a sentence about the picture.

6 _____

Name _____

Write It

Look at the picture.
Then use the words in the box to write a sentence on the lines.

tap Pam I it. see

_____

_____

_____

a fan. cat The ran from

_____

_____

_____

Use the words in the box to write a sentence. Then draw a picture.

rat   nap

_____

_____

_____

Short a Word Families

Write **an**, **at**, **am**, or **ap** to finish each word.

WEEK 3

Home–School Connection

To Parents
This week your child reviewed how to read and write words from the **-an**, **-at**, **-am**, and **-ap** word families.

 c _____

 m _____

 c _____

 m _____

 h _____

 cl _____

 h _____

 cl _____

Read the sentence. Fill in the circle below the correct picture.

1 It is a map.

 ○   ○

2 I see a fan.

  ○    ○

3 It is a hat.

 ○   ○

WEEK 4

-en
-et

Will a Hen Get Wet?

Word Families
-en, -et

Vocabulary
-en: hen, men, pen, ten, then
-et: get, jet, let, met, net, pet, vet, wet, yet

High-Frequency Words: a, am, are, has, I, is, see, the, there, they, we, where

Day 1

SKILLS:
Phonemic Awareness
• Generate sounds from letter patterns
• Blend two to four phonemes into recognizable words

Phonics/ Word Analysis
• Read words with common spelling patterns
• Read high-frequency and sight words
• Read regularly spelled one-syllable words

Comprehension
• Identify story characters
• Identify main idea
• Respond to who, what, where, how questions

Introducing Short *e* Word Families: *-en, -et*

Distribute the Day 1 activity page. Say: *This week we are reading and writing two short* **e** *word families:* **/ĕn/** *and* **/ĕt/**.

• *Point to the* **-en** *box at the top of the page. Say* **/ĕn/**. *(/ĕn/) Point to the first word. Say the letter sounds with me:* **/h-ĕ-n/**. *Blend the sounds together:* **hen**. *Point to the next word:* **/p-ĕ-n/**, **pen**. *Point to the last word:* **/t-ĕ-n/**, **ten**. *What word part is the same in these words? (/ĕn/) These words belong to the* **-en** *word family because they all end with* **en**.

• *Now point to the* **-et** *box. Say* **/ĕt/**. *(/ĕt/) Point to the first word. Say the letter sounds with me:* **/w-ĕ-t/**, **wet**. *Point to the next word:* **/m-ĕ-t/**, **met**. *Point to the last word:* **/g-ĕ-t/**, **get**. *What word part is the same in all of these words? (/ĕt/) These words belong to the* **-et** *word family.*

Listening to the Story

Say: *Listen as I read you a story that has words from the* **-en** *and the* **-et** *word families. The title of this story is "Will a Hen Get Wet?"*

One day, a hen discovered that the pen gate was open. Soon, ten hens were gone! They went down to the pond. Some ducks were playing in the pond. "Hi, Hens. Come in and get wet," quacked the ducks. "We do not like to get wet," clucked the hens. Not like to get wet? The ducks were upset. Everyone likes to get wet!

Thinking About the Story

Distribute pencils. Guide students in discussing the story. Say:

• *The characters in this story are animals. What animals are in the story? (hens, ducks) What word part do you hear at the end of* **hen**? *(-en) Which word family does that word belong to:* **-en** *or* **-et**? *(-en) Make a dot on each of the* **ten hens**.

• *What was this story about? (hens get out of their pen) What did the ducks think the hens would like to do? (get wet in the pond) What word part do you hear at the end of* **get** *and* **wet**? *(-et) Which word family do those words belong to? (-et) Write an* **X** *on one duck.*

Day 1 picture

SKILLS:
Phonemic Awareness
• Generate sounds from letter patterns
• Segment onset and rimes

Phonics/ Word Analysis
• Read words with common spelling patterns
• Read high-frequency and sight words
• Read regularly spelled one-syllable words

Comprehension
• Recall details
• Respond to who, what, where, how questions

Writing
• Print legibly and space letters and words appropriately

Listening for *-en* and *-et* Words

Guide a discussion that helps students recall yesterday's story. Say:

Our story was about hens and ducks. How many hens were there? (ten) *What did they do when the gate was open?* (left their pen)

- *Which word family do the words **hen**, **ten**, and **pen** belong to?* (-en)

Then distribute pencils and the Day 2 activity. Say:

- *Point to the **-en** word family at the top of the page. Let's read the **-en** words together. Point to each word as we read:* **hen, men, pen.**

- *Now point to the **-et** word family at the top of the page. Let's read the **-et** words together. Point to each word as we read:* **net, jet, wet.**

- *Look at number 1. It shows a hen. What is the first sound in **hen**?* (/h/) *Which word part do you hear at the <u>end</u> of **hen**?* (/ĕn/) *Write the word **hen** in the boxes.*

Repeat the process for numbers 2 through 6. Then say:

- *Look at the words at the bottom of the page. Read each word. Circle the words that belong to the **-en** word family. Underline the words that belong to the **-et** word family. Let's read the first word together:* **wet.** *Which word family does **wet** belong to?* (-et) *Draw a line under **wet**.*

Repeat the process for the remaining words.

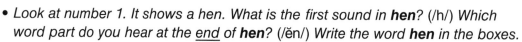

Day 2 activity

SKILLS:
Phonics/ Word Analysis
• Read words with common spelling patterns
• Read high-frequency and sight words
• Read regularly spelled one-syllable words

Comprehension
• Recall details
• Respond to who, what, where, how questions

Writing
• Print legibly and space letters and words appropriately

Writing *-en* and *-et* Sentences

Reread the Day 1 story. Then guide a discussion about the story by saying:

Our story was about ten hens. The hens did not want to do something. What was it? (get wet) *Which word family do **get** and **wet** belong to?* (-et)

Distribute pencils and the Day 3 activity. Say:

*We are going to read, trace, and then write sentences that have **-en** and **-et** words.*

- *Point to the first sentence. Move your finger under each word as we read together:* **See the hen.** *Which word is from the **-en** word family?* (hen) *Now trace the sentence, then write the sentence again on the line below. Put your pencil down when you are finished.*

- *Point to the next sentence. Let's read it together:* **Are there ten?** *Which word is from the **-en** word family?* (ten) *Trace the sentence, then write the sentence again on the line below. Put your pencil down when you are finished.*

After students complete sentence 2, have them read sentences 1 and 2 aloud. Repeat the process for sentences 3 and 4.

Day 3 activity

SKILLS:
**Phonics/
Word Analysis**
- Read words with common spelling patterns
- Read high-frequency and sight words
- Read regularly spelled one-syllable words

Comprehension
- Recall details
- Respond to who, what, where, how questions

Writing
- Print legibly and space letters and words appropriately

Reading *-en* and *-et* Words

Reread the Day 1 story if necessary. Then guide a discussion about the story by saying:

*Our story was about hens and ducks. How many hens got out of the pen? (ten) What word family does **ten** belong to? (-en)*

- *What did the hens not like to do? (get wet) What word family does **wet** belong to? (-et)*

Distribute pencils and the Day 4 activity. Say:

Listen carefully and follow my directions.

- *Put your finger on the first sentence at the top of the page. Move your finger under each word as we read it together: **Ben has ten**. Underline the words from the **-en** word family. (Ben, ten) Draw a line to the picture that matches the sentence.*

Repeat the process for numbers 2 through 4. Then point to the word box at the bottom of the page and say:

- *Point to this word box. Let's read the words together: **vet**, **ten**, **wet**. Each sentence below is missing one word. Look at the picture next to each sentence. Write one of the words from the word box to complete each sentence.*

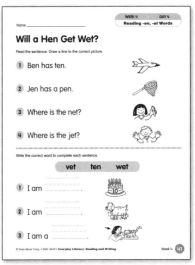

Day 4 activity

Oral Language Activity

SKILLS:
**Phonemic
Awareness**
- Recognize a new spoken word when a phoneme is added, changed, or removed

**Phonics/
Word Analysis**
- Read words with common spelling patterns

Reinforce this week's word families by using a phoneme substitution activity. Introduce and model the call-and-response below.

All: *Let's make a word family; we'll have fun.*
All: *Let's make a word family; **-et** is one.*

Students: *What's the word?*
Teacher: *The word is **wet**.*
Students: *What do we change?*
Teacher: *Change /w/ to /p/.*
Students: ***Pet!***
Teacher: ***Pet** is the word.*

Students: *What's the word?*
Teacher: *The word is **pet**.*
Students: *What do we change?*
Teacher: *Change /p/ to /m/.*
Students: ***Met!***
Teacher: ***Met** is the word.*

Continue the chant using ***get**, **let**, **set**, **yet**.*

Then repeat the chant using **-en** family words: */t/ ten, /p/ pen, /h/ hen, /th/ then, /wh/ when, /m/ men,* etc.

Extension: Write **-et** and **-en** words on index cards. Recite the chant above using letter names instead of sounds. For example, say: *Change **p** to **m**.* After students say the new word, hold up the corresponding word card (**met**) as you say the word.

Will a Hen Get Wet?

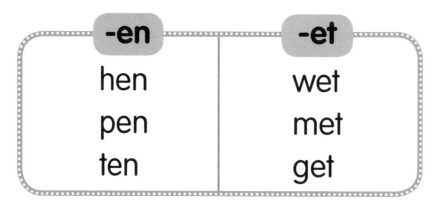

-en	-et
hen	wet
pen	met
ten	get

Name _____

Will a Hen Get Wet?

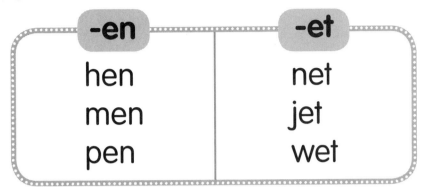

-en	**-et**
hen	net
men	jet
pen	wet

Write the correct word in the boxes.

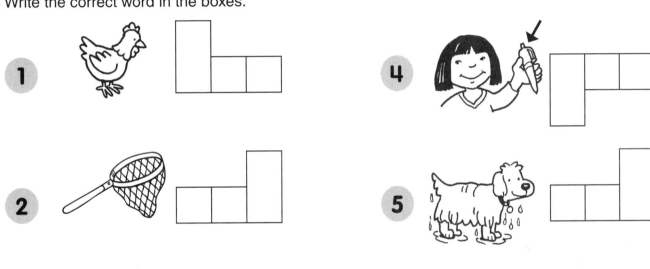

1

2

3

4

5

6

Circle the **-en** words. Underline the **-et** words.

-en	-et

wet   pen   get   hen   set   then

yet   pet   ten   met   vet   let

Name _____

Will a Hen Get Wet?

Read the sentence. Trace the sentence. Then write the sentence on the line below.

1 See the hen.

2 Are there ten?

3 We met ducks.

4 They get wet.

Will a Hen Get Wet?

Read the sentence. Draw a line to the correct picture.

1 Ben has ten.

2 Jen has a pen.

3 Where is the net?

4 Where is the jet?

Write the correct word to complete each sentence.

vet   ten   wet

1 I am _____ .

2 I am _____ .

3 I am a _____ .

Name _____

Will a Hen Get Wet?

What to Do
Read the story with your child and look at the picture together. Then have your child circle words in the story that end with **-en** and draw a line under words that end with **-et**.

"Come and get wet!" said the ducks.

"We do not like to get wet," said the ten hens.

"What? Everyone likes to get wet!" said the ducks.

What to Do Next
Work together with your child to write a story using words from the **-en** and **-et** word families.

Everyday Literacy: Reading and Writing • EMC 2419 • © Evan-Moor Corp.

WEEK 5
-ell
-ed

Nell and the Red Sled

Word Families
-ell, -ed
Vocabulary
-ell: bell, fell, Nell, sell, shell, spell, tell, well, yell
-ed: bed, fed, red, shed, sled, sped, Ted
High-Frequency Words: a, have, hear, her, I, in, is, me, my, on, the, to

Day 1

SKILLS:
Phonemic Awareness
• Generate sounds from letter patterns
• Blend two to four phonemes into recognizable words

Phonics/ Word Analysis
• Read words with common spelling patterns
• Read high-frequency and sight words
• Read regularly spelled one-syllable words

Comprehension
• Identify story characters
• Identify main idea
• Respond to who, what, where, how questions

Introducing Short *e* Word Families: *-ell, -ed*

Distribute the Day 1 activity page. Say: *This week we are reading and writing two more short* **e** *word families: /ĕll/ and /ĕd/.*

• *Point to the* **-ell** *box at the top of the page. Say /ĕll/. (/ĕll/) Point to the first word. Say the letter sounds with me: /f-ĕ-ll. Blend the sounds together:* **fell**. *Point to the next word:* /y-ĕ-l/, **yell**. *Point to the last word:* /n-ĕ-l/, **Nell**. *What word part is the same in all of these words? (/ell/) These words belong to the* **-ell** *word family.*

• *Now point to the* **-ed** *box. Say /ĕd/. (/ĕd/) Point to the first word. Say the letter sounds with me: /r-ĕ-d/,* **red**. *Point to the next word:* /s-l-ĕ-d/, **sled**. *Point to the last word:* /s-p-ĕ-d/, **sped**. *What word part is the same in all of these words? (/ed/) These words belong to the* **-ed** *word family.*

Listening to the Story

Say: *Listen as I read you a story that has words from the* **-ell** *and the* **-ed** *word families. The title of this story is "Nell and the Red Sled."*

Last night it snowed. This morning, I got my red sled from the shed. My dog Nell and I went to the park. We pulled the sled to the top of the hill. Then I got on. I gave a yell as I sped on my sled. Nell chased me all the way. At the bottom of the hill, I fell into the snow. Nell jumped onto the sled and barked. She wanted to ride on the red sled, too!

Thinking About the Story

Distribute pencils. Guide students in discussing the story. Say:

• *Who are the characters in this story? (a girl and her dog Nell) What word part do you hear at the end of* **Nell**, **yell**, **fell**? *(/ĕl/) Which word family do those words belong to:* **-ed** *or* **-ell**? *(-ell) Make a dot on* **Nell** *and the girl who* **fell**.

• *What was this story about? (fun in the snow) What did the characters do for fun? (sped down a hill on a red sled) What word part do you hear at the end of* **sped**, **red**, *and* **sled**? *(/ĕd/) Which word family do those words belong to? (-ed) Write an* **X** *beside the* **sled**.

Day 1 picture

SKILLS:

Phonemic Awareness
• Generate sounds from letter patterns
• Segment onset and rimes

Phonics/ Word Analysis
• Read words with common spelling patterns
• Read high-frequency and sight words
• Read regularly spelled one-syllable words

Comprehension
• Recall details
• Respond to who, what, where, how questions

Writing
• Print legibly and space letters and words appropriately

Listening for -*ell* and -*ed* Words

Guide a discussion that helps students recall yesterday's story. Say:

Our story was about riding a sled.

• *What did the girl do the morning after it snowed?* (took her sled from the shed; sped down the hill)

• *Which word family do the words **sled**, **shed**, and **sped** belong to?* (-ed)

Then distribute pencils and the Day 2 activity. Say:

• *Point to the **-ell** word family at the top of the page. Let's read the **-ell** words together. Point to each word as we read: **yell**, **bell**, **well**.*

• *Now point to the **-ed** word family at the top of the page. Let's read the **-ed** words together. Point to each word as we read: **bed**, **shed**, **sled**.*

• *Look at number 1. It shows a bell. What is the first sound in **bell**?* (/b/) *Which word part do you hear at the <u>end</u> of **bell**?* (/ĕl/) *Write the word **bell** in the boxes.*

Repeat the process for numbers 2 through 6. Then say:

• *Look at the words at the bottom of the page. Read each word. Circle the words that belong to the **-ell** word family. Underline the words that belong to the **-ed** word family. Let's read the first word together: **red**. Which word family does **red** belong to?* (-ed) *Draw a line under **red**.*

Repeat the process for the remaining words.

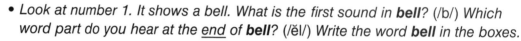

Day 2 activity

SKILLS:

Phonics/ Word Analysis
• Read words with common spelling patterns
• Read high-frequency and sight words
• Read regularly spelled one-syllable words

Comprehension
• Recall details
• Respond to who, what, where, how questions

Writing
• Print legibly and space letters and words appropriately

Writing -*ell* and -*ed* Sentences

Reread the Day 1 story. Then guide a discussion about the story by saying:

In our story, a dog and a girl go down a hill. What was the dog's name? (Nell) *What happened at the bottom of the hill?* (the girl fell) *Which word family do the words **Nell** and **fell** belong to?* (-ell)

Distribute pencils and the Day 3 activity. Say:

*We are going to read, trace, and then write sentences that have -**ell** and -**ed** words.*

• *Point to the first sentence. Move your finger under each word as we read together: **My sled is red**. Which words are from the -**ed** word family?* (sled, red) *Now trace the sentence, then write the sentence again on the line below. Put your pencil down when you are finished.*

Day 3 activity

• *Point to the next sentence. Let's read it together: **I sped on a sled**. Which words are from the -**ed** word family?* (sped, sled) *Trace the sentence, then write the sentence again on the line below. Put your pencil down when you are finished.*

After students complete sentence 2, have them read sentences 1 and 2 aloud. Repeat the process for sentences 3 and 4.

Day 4

SKILLS:

**Phonics/
Word Analysis**
- Read words with common spelling patterns
- Read high-frequency and sight words
- Read regularly spelled one-syllable words

Comprehension
- Recall details
- Respond to who, what, where, how questions

Writing
- Print legibly and space letters and words appropriately

Reading *-ell* and *-ed* Words

Reread the Day 1 story if necessary. Then guide a discussion about the story by saying:

What did the girl in our story do as she sped down the hill? (yell) *What happened at the bottom of the hill?* (she fell)

- *What word family do **yell** and **fell** belong to?* (-ell)

Distribute pencils and the Day 4 activity. Say:
Listen carefully and follow my directions.

- *Put your finger on the first sentence at the top of the page. Move your finger under each word as we read it together: **The sled is red**. Underline the words from the -ed word family. (sled, red) Draw a line to the picture that matches the sentence.*

Repeat the process for numbers 2 through 4. Then point to the word box at the bottom of the page and say:

- *Point to this word box. Let's read the words together: **bell**, **sled**, **shell**. Each sentence below is missing one word. Look at the picture next to each sentence. Write one of the words from the word box to complete each sentence.*

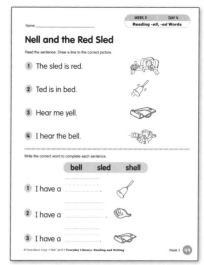

Day 4 activity

Day 5

SKILLS:

Phonemic Awareness
- Recognize a new spoken word when a phoneme is added, changed, or removed

**Phonics/
Word Analysis**
- Read words with common spelling patterns

Oral Language Activity

Reinforce this week's word families by using a phoneme substitution activity. Introduce and model the call-and-response below.

All: *Let's make a word family; we'll have fun.*
All: *Let's make a word family; **-ed** is one.*

Students: *What's the word?*
Teacher: *The word is **red**.*
Students: *What do we change?*
Teacher: *Change **/r/** to **/b/**.*
Students: ***Bed**!*
Teacher: ***Bed** is the word.*

Students: *What's the word?*
Teacher: *The word is **bed**.*
Students: *What do we change?*
Teacher: *Change **/b/** to **/sh/**.*
Students: ***Shed**!*
Teacher: ***Shed** is the word.*

Continue the chant using ***fed**, **sped**, **Ted**, **led***.

Then repeat the chant using **-ell** family words: */b/ bell, /f/ fell, /t/ tell, /sh/ shell, /w/ well, /d/ dell*, etc.

Extension: Write -ed and -ell words on index cards. Recite the chant above using letter names instead of sounds. For example, say: *Change **b** to **sh**.* After students say the new word, hold up the corresponding word card (**shed**) as you say the word.

Home–School Connection p. 50
Spanish version available (see p. 2)

Nell and the Red Sled

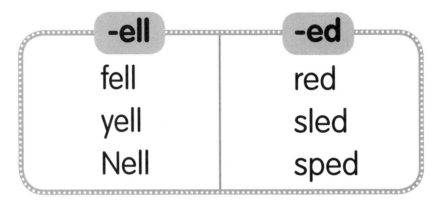

-ell	**-ed**
fell	red
yell	sled
Nell	sped

Name _____

Nell and the Red Sled

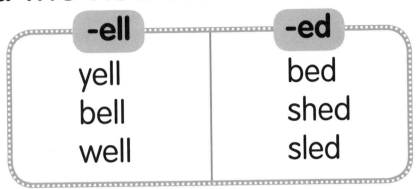

-ell	-ed
yell	bed
bell	shed
well	sled

Write the correct word in the boxes.

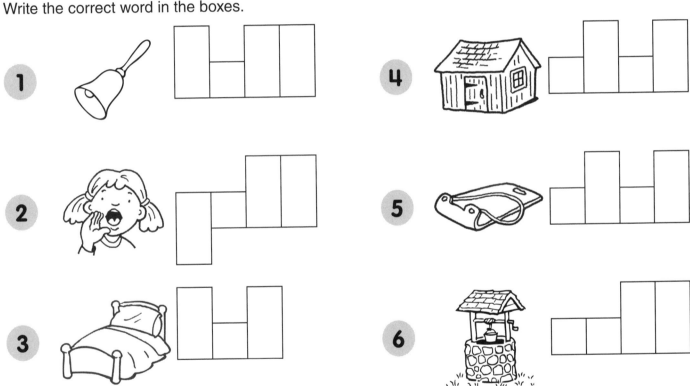

1

2

3

4

5

6

Circle the **-ell** words. Underline the **-ed** words.

(-ell) _-ed_

red	sell	bell	sled	bed	spell
fell	fed	Ted	tell	well	shell

Nell and the Red Sled

Read the sentence. Trace the sentence. Then write the sentence on the line below.

1 My sled is red.

2 I sped on a sled.

3 I yell to Nell.

4 I tell her I fell.

Nell and the Red Sled

Read the sentence. Draw a line to the correct picture.

1 The sled is red.

2 Ted is in bed.

3 Hear me yell.

4 I hear the bell.

Write the correct word to complete each sentence.

bell   sled   shell

1 I have a _____ .

2 I have a _____ .

3 I have a _____ .

Name _____

Nell and the Red Sled

What to Do
Read the story with your child and look at the picture together.
Then have your child circle words in the story that end with **-ell**
and draw a line under words that end with **-ed**.

WEEK 5

Home–School Connection

To Parents
This week your child learned to read and write words from the **-ell** and **-ed** word families.

My red sled was in the shed.
I sped down the hill on my sled.
I gave a yell. Then I fell! It was fun.

What to Do Next
Work together with your child to write a story using words from the **-ell** and **-ed** word families.

Review It

Short *e* Word Family Words:

-en: hen, pen, ten
-et: get, jet, let, net, pet, vet, wet, yet
-ell: bell, Nell, sell, shell, spell, well, yell
-ed: bed, fed, red, shed, sled, sped, Ted

High-Frequency Words: a, gave, get, have, hear, I, is, like, my, not, on, to the, this, where, will

Day 1

SKILLS:
Phonemic Awareness
• Generate sounds from letter patterns
• Blend two to four phonemes into recognizable words

Phonics/Word Analysis
• Read words with common spelling patterns
• Read regularly spelled one-syllable words

Listening for Short *e* Word Families

Distribute the Day 1 activity and a pencil to each student. Then say:

• *Let's review the short* **e** *word families we learned during the past few weeks. Point to each gray box as we read each word family ending together:* **-en, -et, -ed, -ell.** *Now we'll match each picture to its word family. Point to the jet. Say* **jet.** *(jet) What word family does* **jet** *belong to? (-et) What letters stand for /ĕt/? (et) Draw a line from the jet to the correct word family.*

• *Point to the bed. Say* **bed.** *(bed) What word family does* **bed** *belong to? (-ed) What letters stand for /ĕd/? (ed) Draw a line from the bed to the correct word family.*

• *Point to the ten. Say* **ten.** *(ten) What word family does* **ten** *belong to? (-en) What letters stand for /ĕn/? Draw a line from the ten to the correct word family.*

Repeat the process for the remaining picture words: **bell, sled, net, shed,** and **shell.**

Discriminating *-en, -et, -ed, -ell*

Direct students' attention to the bottom half of the page. Say:

• *These words belong to short* **e** *word families. We're going to read each word and follow the directions shown in the box. Let's start with the* **-en** *word family. When you read a word that belongs to the* **-en** *family, draw a circle around it. Do that now. (pause) Which words did you circle? (ten, hen, pen)*

• *Now look for words from the* **-et** *word family. When you read a word that belongs to the* **-et** *family, draw a box around it. Do that now. (pause) Which words did you box? (yet, jet, let, vet, get)*

• *Now look for words from the* **-ed** *word family. When you read a word that belongs to the* **-ed** *family, draw a line under it. Do that now. (pause) Which words did you underline? (red, Ted, fed)*

• *Now look for words from the* **-ell** *word family. When you read a word that belongs to the* **-ell** *family, write an* **X** *above it. Do that now. (pause) Which words did you mark with an* **X***? (sell, Nell, spell, yell)*

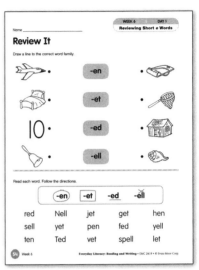

Day 1 activity

Day 2

SKILLS:

Phonemic Awareness
- Segment onset and rime

Phonics/ Word Analysis
- Read words with common spelling patterns
- Read high-frequency and sight words
- Read regularly spelled one-syllable words

Writing
- Print legibly and space letters and words appropriately

Writing Short *e* Word Family Words

Distribute the Day 2 activity and a pencil to each student. Then say:

- *Look at the word endings in the box. Let's read them together: -en, -et, -ed, -ell. Now look at the pictures below.*

- *Point to picture number 1. It shows a bed. Which word family does **bed** belong to? (-ed) Write the missing letters to finish the word **bed**.*

- *Point to picture number 2. It shows a bell. Which word family does **bell** belong to? (-ell) Write the missing letters to finish the word **bell**.*

Repeat the process for the remaining words: **shed, shell, pen, pet, wet, well.** Then say:

- *Now we're going to read sentences and draw a line to the matching picture. Point to number 1. Let's read together: **A duck will get wet. The hen will not.** Draw a line to the picture that matches.*

Repeat the process for the remaining sentences.

Day 2 activity

Day 3

SKILLS:

Phonics/ Word Analysis
- Read words with common spelling patterns
- Read high-frequency and sight words
- Read regularly spelled one-syllable words

Writing
- Use developing knowledge of letter-sound correspondences to spell independently
- Print legibly and space letters and words appropriately

Reading Words with *-en, -et, -ed, -ell*

Distribute the Day 3 activity and a pencil to each student. Say:

- *The words in the box belong to short **e** word families. Point to each word and read with me: **jet, pen, bell, red, sled, wet, ten, net, hen, well.***

- *Point to sentence number 1. Move your finger under each word as we read together: **I have a red (blank).** What does the picture show? (sled) Write **sled** to complete the sentence. Use the word box if you need help.*

- *Read sentence 2: **I hear a (blank).** What does the picture show? (bell) Write **bell** in the sentence.*

- *Read sentence 3: **Ted is (blank).** What does the picture show? (ten) Write **ten** in the sentence.*

- *Read sentence 4: **I get (blank).** What does the picture show? (wet) Write **wet** in the sentence.*

- *Read sentence 5: **Where is the (blank)?** What does the picture show? (hen) Write **hen** in the sentence.*

- *Now let's read all of the sentences together. Move your finger under each word as we read. Number 1: **I have a red sled.** 2. **I hear a bell.** 3. **Ted is ten.** 4. **I get wet.** 5. **Where is the hen?***

- *Point to number 6. What do you see in the picture? (a girl holding a pen) Write a sentence about the picture. (Answers vary.) Then read your sentence to a classmate.*

Day 3 activity

SKILLS:

**Phonics/
Word Analysis**
- Read words with common spelling patterns
- Read high-frequency and sight words
- Read regularly spelled one-syllable words

Comprehension
- Describe a picture using complete sentences

Writing
- Use developing knowledge of letter-sound correspondences to spell independently
- Print legibly and space letters and words appropriately

Writing Short *e* Word Sentences

Distribute the Day 4 activity and pencils. Say:

Day 4 activity

- *Look at the first picture. What do you see?* (a hen beside a pond) *Now look at the words in the first box. These words make up a sentence that tells about the picture. The words are out of order. Unscramble the words to write a sentence about the picture. Put your pencil down when you are finished.*

- *Look at the next picture. What do you see?* (a dog speeding down a hill on a sled) *Now look at the words in the box. These words make up a sentence that tells about the picture. The words are out of order. Unscramble the words to write a sentence about the picture. Put your pencil down when you are finished.*

- *Look at the words in the last box. Point to each word as we read it:* **hen**, **red***. Write a sentence that uses these words. Then draw a picture about your sentence.* (Answers vary.)

SKILLS:

**Phonics/
Word Analysis**
- Read words with common spelling patterns
- Use context clues in decoding words

Phonics Game

Review the short **e** word families students learned this week by playing the following game.

Materials: 4 index cards per group, labeled **-en**, **-et**, **-ed**, and **-ell**

Preparation: Divide the class into groups of four. Give each group a set of word family cards.

How to Play: Pick a "mystery word" from the chart below and write its first letter (or blend) on the board. Have students in each group sort through their word family cards and find all the cards that can be added to that letter to form a word. For example, if you write **b** on the board, students should determine that they can form **Ben**, **bet**, **bed**, and **bell**.

Then give students the mystery word's clue from the chart, and have each group decide what the mystery word is (e.g., "something you sleep in" must be "bed") and the word family card that can be used to form it (**-ed**). Ask a volunteer from each group to hold up the correct card.

Mystery Word	Clue	Mystery Word	Clue
bed	something you sleep in	**Jen**	a girl's name
men	more than one man	**net**	you use it to catch a frog
pet	a hamster in a cage is a _____	**Ted**	a boy's name
well	you can make a wish in a _____	**spell**	you write letters to _____ a word

Name _____

Review It

Draw a line to the correct word family.

 •

 •   -en   •

 •

 •   -et   •

  •

10 •   -ed   •

 •

 •   -ell   •

Read each word. Follow the directions.

red	Nell	jet	get	hen
sell	yet	pen	fed	yell
ten	Ted	vet	spell	let

Name _____

Write It

Which word family do you hear?
Write **en**, **et**, **ed**, or **ell** to spell each word.

-en   -et   -ed   -ell

1  b _____

2  b _____

3  sh _____

4  sh _____

5  p _____

6  p _____

7  w _____

8 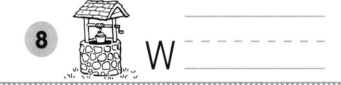 w _____

Read the sentences. Draw a line to the correct picture.

1   A duck will get wet.
    The hen will not.

2   I sped on my sled.
    I gave a yell to Nell.

© Evan-Moor Corp. • EMC 2419 • *Everyday Literacy: Reading and Writing*   Week 6   55

Name _____

Read It

Read the words in the box. Write the correct word to complete each sentence.

jet	pen	bell	red	sled
wet	ten	net	hen	well

1 I have a red _____.

2 I hear a _____.

3 Ted is _____.

4 I get _____.

5 Where is the _____?

Write a sentence about the picture.

6 _____

Write It

Look at the picture.
Then use the words in the box to write a sentence on the lines.

wet? hen get Will the

_____

Nell my sled. sped on

_____

Use the words in the box to write a sentence. Then draw a picture.

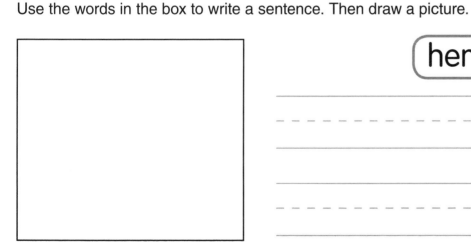

hen red

_____

Name _____

Short e Word Families

Write **en**, **et**, **ed**, or **ell** to finish each word.

To Parents
This week your child reviewed how to read and write words belonging to short **e** word families: **-en**, **-et**, **-ed**, and **-ell**.

b _____

b _____

r _____

10 t _____

p _____

p _____

w _____

w _____

Read the sentence. Fill in the circle below the correct picture.

1 I have a pet.

○   ○

2 I have a bell.

○   ○

3 I like this shell.

○   ○

Everyday Literacy: Reading and Writing • EMC 2419 • © Evan-Moor Corp.

Can Miss Pig Win?

WEEK 7

-ig
-in

Word Families
-ig, -in
Vocabulary
-ig: big, dig, fig, jig, pig, twig, wig
-in: chin, fin, grin, in, pin, thin, tin, twin, win
High-Frequency Words: a, and, have, I, is, on, take, this, try

Day 1

SKILLS:

Phonemic Awareness
• Generate sounds from letter patterns
• Blend two to four phonemes into recognizable words

Phonics/ Word Analysis
• Read words with common spelling patterns
• Read high-frequency and sight words
• Read regularly spelled one-syllable words

Comprehension
• Identify story characters
• Identify main idea
• Respond to who, what, where, how questions

Introducing Short *i* Word Families: *-ig, -in*

Distribute the Day 1 activity page. Say: *This week we are reading and writing two short **i** word families: /ĭg/ and /ĭn/.*

• *Point to the **-ig** box at the top of the page. Say /ĭg/. (/ĭg/) Point to the first word. Say the letter sounds with me: /b-ĭ-g/. Blend the sounds together: **big**. Point to the next word: /f-ĭ-g/, **fig**. Point to the last word: /p-ĭ-g/, **pig**. What word part is the same in all of these words? (/ĭg/) These words belong to the **-ig** word family because they all end with **ig**.*

• *Now point to the **-in** box. Say /ĭn/. (/ĭn/) Point to the first word. Say the letter sounds with me: /w-ĭ-n/, **win**. Point to the next word: /th-ĭ-n/, **thin**. Point to the last word: /g-r-ĭ-n/, **grin**. What word part is the same in all of these words? (/ĭn/) These words belong to the **-in** word family.*

Listening to the Story

Say: *Listen as I read you a story that has words from the **-ig** and the **-in** word families. The title of this story is "Can Miss Pig Win?"*

Miss Pig wanted to win "best pig" at the fair. Then she could wear a big pin. But she was too thin to win. Miss Pig saw a fig tree. She had an idea. She put the figs in her basket and went home with a grin. She made fig jam. It was good! She ate it on everything. Did the jam make her big? Did she win best pig? No, but she did win "best fig"— best fig jam! Miss Pig wore her big pin with a grin!

Thinking About the Story

Distribute pencils. Guide students in discussing the story. Say:

• *Who is the character in this story? (Miss Pig) How does she win? (by making fig jam) What word part do you hear at the end of **pig** and **fig**? (/ĭg/) Which word family do those words belong to: **-ig** or **-in**? (-ig) Make a dot on Miss **Pig** and a **fig**.*

• *What was this story about? (how a thin pig wins) What word part do you hear at the end of **thin** and **win**? (/ĭn/) Which word family do those words belong to? (-in) Write an **X** beside something that might make Miss Pig **grin**.*

Day 1 picture

SKILLS:

Phonemic Awareness

• Generate sounds from letter patterns

• Segment onset and rime

Phonics/ Word Analysis

• Read words with common spelling patterns

• Read high-frequency and sight words

• Read regularly spelled one-syllable words

Comprehension

• Recall details

• Respond to who, what, where, how questions

Writing

• Print legibly and space letters and words appropriately

Listening for *-ig* and *-in* Words

Guide a discussion that helps students recall yesterday's story. Say:

In our story, Miss Pig was not very big.

- *How did she win a prize at the fair?* (made fig jam)
- *Which word family do the words **pig**, **big**, and **fig** belong to?* (-ig)

Then distribute pencils and the Day 2 activity. Say:

- *Point to the **-ig** word family at the top of the page. Let's read the **-ig** words together. Point to each word as we read: **big**, **wig**, **dig**.*
- *Now point to the **-in** word family at the top of the page. Let's read the **-in** words together. Point to each word as we read: **pin**, **win**, **chin**.*
- *Look at number 1. It shows a wig. What is the first sound in **wig**?* (/w/) *Which word part do you hear at the <u>end</u> of **wig**?* (/ĭg/) *Write the word **wig** in the boxes.*

Repeat the process for numbers 2 through 6. Then say:

- *Look at the words at the bottom of the page. Read each word. Circle the words that belong to the **-ig** word family. Underline the words that belong to the **-in** word family. Let's read the first word together: **fig**. Which word family does **fig** belong to?* (-ig) *Circle the word **fig**.*

Repeat the process for the remaining words.

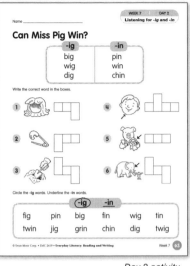

Day 2 activity

SKILLS:

Phonics/ Word Analysis

• Read words with common spelling patterns

• Read high-frequency and sight words

• Read regularly spelled one-syllable words

Comprehension

• Recall details

• Respond to who, what, where, how questions

Writing

• Print legibly and space letters and words appropriately

Writing *-ig* and *-in* Sentences

Reread the Day 1 story. Then guide a discussion about the story by saying:

Our story was about a pig that wanted to win. What did Miss Pig win that made her grin? (a pin)

- *Which word family do the words **win**, **pin**, and **grin** belong to?* (-in)

Distribute pencils and the Day 3 activity. Say:

*We are going to read, trace, and then write sentences that have **-ig** and **-in** words.*

- *Point to the first sentence. Move your finger under each word as we read together: **Is this pig big?** Which words are from the **-ig** word family?* (pig, big) *Now trace the sentence, then write the sentence again on the line below. Put your pencil down when you are finished.*
- *Point to the next sentence. Let's read it together: **This pig is thin.** Which word is from the **-in** word family?* (thin) *Trace the sentence, then write the sentence again on the line below. Put your pencil down when you are finished.*

After students complete sentence 2, have them read sentences 1 and 2 aloud. Repeat the process for sentences 3 and 4.

Day 3 activity

SKILLS:
**Phonics/
Word Analysis**
• Read words with
common spelling
patterns
• Read high-frequency
and sight words
• Read regularly
spelled one-syllable
words
Comprehension
• Recall details
• Respond to who,
what, where, how
questions
Writing
• Print legibly and
space letters and
words appropriately

Reading *-ig* and *-in* Words

Reread the Day 1 story if necessary. Then guide a discussion about the story by saying:

There was a thin pig in our story.

• *What did Miss Pig make?* (fig jam)
• *What word family is the word **fig** from?* (-ig)
• *What did Miss Pig win?* (a pin)
• *What word family is **pin** from?* (-in)

Distribute pencils and the Day 4 activity. Say:

Listen carefully and follow my directions.

• *Put your finger on the first sentence at the top of the page. Move your finger under each word as we read it together: **I have a fin**. Underline the word from the **-in** word family. (fin) Draw a line to the picture that matches the sentence.*

Repeat the process for numbers 2 through 4. Then point to the word box at the bottom of the page and say:

• *Point to this word box. Let's read the words together: **wig**, **swig**, **fig**. Each sentence below is missing one word. Look at the picture next to each sentence. Write one of the words from the word box to complete each sentence.*

Day 4 activity

SKILLS:
**Phonemic
Awareness**
• Recognize a new
spoken word when a
phoneme is added,
changed, or removed
**Phonics/
Word Analysis**
• Read words with
common spelling
patterns

Oral Language Activity

Reinforce this week's word families by using a phoneme substitution activity. Introduce and model the call-and-response below.

All: *Let's make a word family; we'll have fun.*
All: *Let's make a word family; **-ig** is one.*

Students: *What's the word?*
Teacher: *The word is **dig**.*
Students: *What do we change?*
Teacher: *Change /d/ to /w/.*
Students: ***Wig!***
Teacher: ***Wig** is the word.*

Students: *What's the word?*
Teacher: *The word is **wig**.*
Students: *What do we change?*
Teacher: *Change /w/ to /f/.*
Students: ***Fig!***
Teacher: ***Fig** is the word.*

Continue the chant using **pig**, **big**, **jig**, **twig**.

Then repeat the chant using **-in** family words: /f/ fin, /gr/ grin, /tw/ twin, /w/ win, /b/ bin, /k/ kin, etc.

Extension: Write **-ig** and **-in** words on index cards. Recite the chant above using letter names, instead of sounds. For example, say: *Change **w** to **f**.* After students say the new word, hold up the corresponding word card (**fig**) as you say the word.

**Home–School
Connection p. 66**
Spanish version
available (see p. 2)

Name _____

Can Miss Pig Win?

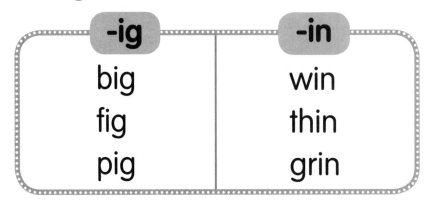

-ig	-in
big	win
fig	thin
pig	grin

Everyday Literacy: Reading and Writing • EMC 2419 • © Evan-Moor Corp.

Name _____

Can Miss Pig Win?

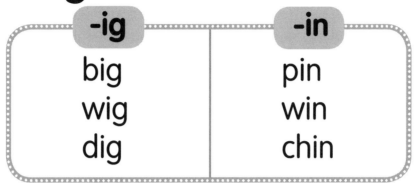

-ig	-in
big	pin
wig	win
dig	chin

Write the correct word in the boxes.

1

2

3

4

5

6

Circle the **-ig** words. Underline the **-in** words.

(-ig)	-in

fig   pin   big   fin   wig   tin

twin   jig   grin   chin   dig   twig

Name _____

Can Miss Pig Win?

Read the sentence. Trace the sentence. Then write the sentence on the line below.

1 Is this pig big?

2 This pig is thin.

3 Eat fig jam.

4 Win a pin.

Everyday Literacy: Reading and Writing • EMC 2419 • © Evan-Moor Corp.

Name _____

Can Miss Pig Win?

Read the sentence. Draw a line to the correct picture.

1 I have a fin.

2 I have a grin.

3 I dig and dig.

4 I jig and jump.

Write the correct word to complete each sentence.

wig   swig   fig

1 Try a _____.

2 Take a _____.

3 Try on a _____.

Name _____

Can Miss Pig Win?

What to Do
Read the story with your child and look at the picture together.
Then have your child circle words in the story that end with **-ig**
and draw a line under words that end with **-in**.

WEEK 7

Home–School Connection

To Parents
This week your child learned to read and write words from the **-ig** and **-in** word families.

Can Miss Pig win at the fair? No, she is a thin pig.
So Miss Pig makes fig jam. She eats to grow big.
Now, see her grin. Miss Pig did win!

What to Do Next
Work together with your child to write a story using words from the **-ig** and **-in** word families.

Let's Knit

Word Families
-ip, -it
Vocabulary
-ip: chip, clip, dip, drip, grip, hip, lip, rip, sip, snip, tip, trip, whip, zip
-it: bit, fit, hit, it, kit, knit, lit, quit, sit
High-Frequency Words: a, can, go, he, it, like, on, she, take, took, we, will, you

WEEK 8
-ip
-it

Day 1

SKILLS:
Phonemic Awareness
• Generate sounds from letter patterns
• Blend two to four phonemes into recognizable words

Phonics/ Word Analysis
• Read words with common spelling patterns
• Read high-frequency and sight words
• Read regularly spelled one-syllable words

Comprehension
• Identify story characters
• Identify main idea
• Respond to who, what, where, how questions

Introducing Short *i* Word Families: *-ip, -it*

Distribute the Day 1 activity page. Say: *This week we are reading and writing two more short **i** word families: /**ĭp**/ and /**ĭt**/.*

• *Point to the **-ip** box at the top of the page. Say /**ĭp**/. (/ĭp/) Point to the first word. Say the letter sounds with me: /**d-ĭ-p**/. Blend the sounds together: **dip**. Point to the next word: /**t-r-ĭ-p**/, **trip**. Point to the last word: /**k-l-ĭ-p**/, **clip**. What word part is the same in all of these words? (/ĭp/) These words belong to the **-ip** word family because they all end with **ip**.*

• *Now point to the **-it** box. Say /**ĭt**/. (/ĭt/) Point to the first word. Say the letter sounds with me: /**k-ĭ-t**/, **kit**. Point to the next word: /**s-ĭ-t**/, **sit**. Point to the last word. The sound of **k** is silent, so you only say the sound of **n**: /**n-ĭ-t**/, **knit**. What word part is the same in all of these words? (/ĭt/) These words belong to the **-it** word family because they all end with **it**.*

Listening to the Story

Say: *Listen as I read you a story that has words from the **-ip** and the **-it** word families. The title of this story is "Let's Knit."*

Gabe and the other first-graders are on a field trip. They are learning how yarn used to be made. Then they will learn how to knit. Gabe watches the farmer grip a sheep. Clip, snip! The sheep loses its wool. The yarn maker washes the wool. She will dip it in colors and hang it up to dry. Drip, drip. Next, she will sit at a spinning wheel and spin it into yarn. Now, Gabe can't wait to knit!

Thinking About the Story

Distribute pencils. Guide students in discussing the story. Say:

• *What did the first-graders learn first?* (how yarn used to be made) *What will they learn next?* (how to knit) *What word part do you hear at the end of **knit**?* (/ĭt/) *Which word family does that word belong to: **-it** or **-ip**?* (-it)

• *Where did the children go?* (on a trip) *What did they see?* (how yarn is made) *What word part do you hear at the end of **trip**, **dip**, **clip**?* (/ĭp/) *Which word family do those words belong to?* (-ip) *Write an **X** beside the person who **clips** the wool.*

Day 1 picture

Day 2

SKILLS:

Phonemic Awareness
- Generate sounds from letter patterns
- Segment onset and rime

Phonics/ Word Analysis
- Read words with common spelling patterns
- Read high-frequency and sight words
- Read regularly spelled one-syllable words

Comprehension
- Recall details
- Respond to who, what, where, how questions

Writing
- Print legibly and space letters and words appropriately

Listening for *-ip* and *-it* Words

Guide a discussion that helps students recall yesterday's story. Say:

Our story was about children who took a field trip.

- *What does the farmer do to get wool?* (clips, snips the sheep's wool)
- *Which word family do the words* **clip** *and* **snip** *belong to?* (-ip)

Then distribute pencils and the Day 2 activity. Say:

- *Point to the* **-ip** *word family at the top of the page. Let's read the* **-ip** *words together. Point to each word as we read:* **rip, chip, lip.**
- *Now point to the* **-it** *word family at the top of the page. Let's read the* **-it** *words together. Point to each word as we read:* **sit, hit, bit.**
- *Look at number 1. It shows a rip. What is the first sound in* **rip**? (/r/) *Which word part do you hear at the <u>end</u> of* **rip**? (/ĭp/) *Write the word* **rip** *in the boxes.*

Repeat the process for numbers 2 through 6. Then say:

- *Look at the words at the bottom of the page. Read each word. Circle the words that belong to the* **-ip** *word family. Underline the words that belong to the* **-it** *word family. Let's read the first word together:* **kit.** *Which word family does* **kit** *belong to?* (-it) *Draw a line under* **kit.**

Repeat the process for the remaining words.

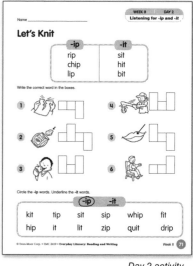

Day 2 activity

Day 3

SKILLS:

Phonics/ Word Analysis
- Read words with common spelling patterns
- Read high-frequency and sight words
- Read regularly spelled one-syllable words

Comprehension
- Recall details
- Respond to who, what, where, how questions

Writing
- Print legibly and space letters and words appropriately

Writing *-ip* and *-it* Sentences

Reread the Day 1 story. Then guide a discussion about the story by saying:

Our story was about Gabe and the other first-graders.

- *What did the children learn to do?* (knit) *Which word family does the word* **knit** *belong to?* (-it)

Distribute pencils and the Day 3 activity. Say:

We are going to read, trace, and then write sentences that have **-ip** *and* **-it** *words.*

- *Point to the first sentence. Move your finger under each word as we read together:* **He will clip.** *Which word is from the* **-ip** *word family?* (clip) *Now trace the sentence, then write the sentence again on the line below. Put your pencil down when you are finished.*
- *Point to the next sentence. Let's read it together:* **She will dip it.** *Which word is from the* **-ip** *word family?* (dip) *Trace the sentence, then write the sentence again on the line below. Put your pencil down when you are finished.*

After students complete sentence 2, have them read sentences 1 and 2 aloud. Repeat the process for sentences 3 and 4. Remind students that the **k** in **knit** is silent.

Day 3 activity

Day 4

SKILLS:

**Phonics/
Word Analysis**

• Read words with common spelling patterns

• Read high-frequency and sight words

Comprehension

• Recall details

• Respond to who, what, where, how questions

Writing

• Print legibly and space letters and words appropriately

Reading *-ip* and *-it* Words

Reread the Day 1 story if necessary. Then guide a discussion about the story by saying:

The children saw how wool is made into yarn.

- *How can wool be colored? (dip it in color) What word family is the word **dip** from? (-ip)*

- *What did the children do with yarn? (knit) What word family is **knit** from? (-it)*

Distribute pencils and the Day 4 activity. Say:

Listen carefully and follow my directions.

- *Put your finger on the first sentence at the top of the page. Move your finger under each word as we read it together: **It likes to sit.** Underline the word from the **-it** word family. (sit) Draw a line to the picture that matches the sentence.*

Repeat the process for numbers 2 through 4. Then point to the word box at the bottom of the page and say:

- *Point to this word box. Let's read the words together: **sit**, **trip**, **ship**. Each sentence below is missing one word. Look at the picture next to each sentence. Write one of the words from the word box to complete each sentence.*

Day 4 activity

Oral Language Activity

Reinforce this week's word families by using a phoneme substitution activity. Introduce and model the call-and-response below.

All: *Let's make a word family; we'll have fun.*
All: *Let's make a word family; **-ip** is one.*

Students: *What's the word?*
Teacher: *The word is **tip**.*
Students: *What do we change?*
Teacher: *Change /t/ to /s/.*
Students: ***Sip!***
Teacher: ***Sip** is the word.*

Students: *What's the word?*
Teacher: *The word is **sip**.*
Students: *What do we change?*
Teacher: *Change /s/ to /hw/.*
Students: ***Whip!***
Teacher: ***Whip** is the word.*

Continue the chant using **trip**, **lip**, **flip**, **hip**.

Then repeat the chant using **-it** family words: /b/ bit, /f/ fit, /s/ sit, /h/ hit, /l/ lit, /p/ pit, /n/ knit, etc.

Extension: Write **-ip** and **-it** words on index cards. Recite the chant above using letter names instead of sounds. For example, say: *Change **s** to **wh**.* After students say the new word, hold up the corresponding word card (**whip**) as you say the word.

Day 5

SKILLS:

Phonemic Awareness

• Recognize a new spoken word when a phoneme is added, changed, or removed

**Phonics/
Word Analysis**

• Read words with common spelling patterns

Home–School Connection p. 74
Spanish version available (see p. 2)

Name _____

Let's Knit

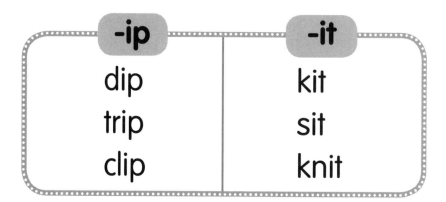

-ip	-it
dip	kit
trip	sit
clip	knit

Name _____

Let's Knit

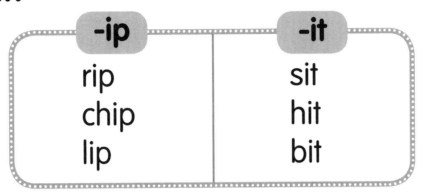

-ip	-it
rip	sit
chip	hit
lip	bit

Write the correct word in the boxes.

1

2

3

4

5

6

Circle the **-ip** words. Underline the **-it** words.

(-ip)	_-it_

kit	tip	sit	sip	whip	fit
hip	it	lit	zip	quit	drip

Name _____

Let's Knit

Read the sentence. Trace the sentence. Then write the sentence on the line below.

1 He will clip it.

2 She will dip it.

3 Gabe can knit it.

4 Will it fit?

Everyday Literacy: Reading and Writing • EMC 2419 • © Evan-Moor Corp.

Name _____

Let's Knit

Read the sentence. Draw a line to the correct picture.

1 It likes to sit.

2 We like to knit.

3 He took a sip.

4 She took a chip.

Write the correct word to complete each sentence.

sit	trip	ship

1 Take a _____ .

2 Go on a _____ .

3 You can _____ .

Name _____

Let's Knit

What to Do
Read the story with your child and look at the picture together.
Then have your child circle words in the story that end with **-ip**
and draw a line under words that end with **-it**.

WEEK 8

Home–School Connection

To Parents
This week your child learned to read and write words from the **-ip** and **-it** word families.

This trip is fun. See him clip and snip.
She will wash the wool. See it drip.
Spin the wool into yarn. Now we can knit!

What to Do Next
Work together with your child to write a story using words from the **-ip** and **-it** word families.

Everyday Literacy: Reading and Writing • EMC 2419 • © Evan-Moor Corp.

Review It

Short *i* Word Family Words:
-ig: big, dig, fig, jig, pig, twig, wig
-in: chin, fin, grin, pin, thin, tin, twin, win
-ip: chip, dip, drip, lip, ship, sip, tip, trip, whip
-it: bit, fit, hit, it, knit, quit, sit

High-Frequency Words: a, did, does, has, he, how, I, is, like, little, my, not, on, that, the, this, to, took, went, where, would, you

---

Day 1

SKILLS:
Phonemic Awareness

• Generate sounds from letter patterns

• Blend two to four phonemes into recognizable words

Phonics/Word Analysis

• Read words with common spelling patterns

• Read regularly spelled one-syllable words

Listening for Short *i* Word Families

Distribute the Day 1 activity and a pencil to each student. Then say:

• *Let's review the short **i** word families we learned during the past few weeks. Point to each gray box as we read each word family ending together: **-ig**, **-in**, **-ip**, **-it**. Now we'll match each picture to its word family. Point to the pin. Say **pin**. (pin) What word family does **pin** belong to? (-in) What letters stand for /ĭn/? (in) Draw a line from the pin to the correct word family.*

• *Point to the wig. Say **wig**. (wig) What word family does **wig** belong to? (-ig) What letters stand for /ĭg/? (ig) Draw a line from the wig to the correct word family.*

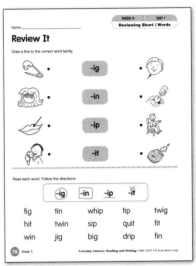

Day 1 activity

• *Point to the lips. Say **lip**. (lip) What word family does **lip** belong to? (-ip) What letters stand for /ĭp/? (ip) Draw a line from the lips to the correct word family.*

Repeat the process for the remaining picture words: **bit**, **chin**, **dig**, **sit**, and **chip**.

Discriminating *-ig, -in, -ip, -it*

Direct students' attention to the bottom half of the page. Then say:

• *These words belong to short **i** word families. We're going to read each word and follow the directions shown in the box. Let's start with the **-ig** word family. When you read a word that belongs to the **-ig** family, draw a circle around it. Do that now. (pause) Which words did you circle? (fig, jig, big, twig)*

• *Now look for words from the **-in** word family. When you read a word that belongs to the **-in** family, draw a box around it. Do that now. (pause) Which words did you box? (win, tin, twin, fin)*

• *Now look for words from the **-ip** word family. When you read a word that belongs to the **-ip** family, draw a line under it. Do that now. (pause) Which words did you underline? (whip, sip, tip, drip)*

• *Now look for words from the **-it** word family. When you read a word that belongs to the **-it** family, write an **X** above it. Do that now. (pause) Which words did you mark with an **X**? (hit, quit, fit)*

Day 2

SKILLS:

Phonemic Awareness

• Segment onset and rime

Phonics/ Word Analysis

• Read words with common spelling patterns

• Read high-frequency and sight words

• Read regularly spelled one-syllable words

Writing

• Print legibly and space letters and words appropriately

Writing Short *i* Word Family Words

Distribute the Day 2 activity and a pencil to each student. Then say:

• *Look at the word endings in the box. Let's read them together: -ig, -in, -ip, -it. Now look at the pictures below.*

• *Point to picture number 1. It shows a wig. Which word family does **wig** belong to? (-ig) Write the missing letters to finish the word **wig**.*

• *Point to picture number 2. It shows something you win. Which word family does **win** belong to? (-in) Write the missing letters to finish the word **win**.*

Repeat the process for the remaining words: **sip**, **sit**, **dip**, **dig**, **twig**, **twin**. Then say:

• *Now we're going to read sentences and draw a line to the matching picture. Point to number 1. Let's read together: **This pig is thin. Did it win?** Draw a line to the picture that matches the sentences.*

Repeat the process for the remaining sentences.

Day 2 activity

Day 3

SKILLS:

Phonics/ Word Analysis

• Read words with common spelling patterns

• Read high-frequency and sight words

• Read regularly spelled one-syllable words

Writing

• Use developing knowledge of letter-sound correspondences to spell independently

• Print legibly and space letters and words appropriately

Reading Words with *-ig, -in, -ip, -it*

Distribute the Day 3 activity and a pencil to each student. Say:

• *The words in the box belong to short **i** word families. Point to each word and read with me: **fin, ship, dig, pig, win, knit, grin, chip, sip, twin**.*

• *Point to sentence number 1. Move your finger under each word as we read together: **Would you like a (blank)?** What does the picture show? (sip) Write **sip** to complete the sentence. Use the word box if you need help.*

• *Read sentence 2: **This is how to (blank).** What does the picture show? (knit) Write **knit** in the sentence.*

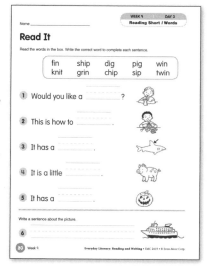

Day 3 activity

• *Read sentence 3: **It has a (blank).** What does the picture show? (fin) Write **fin** in the sentence.*

• *Read sentence 4: **It is a little (blank).** What does the picture show? (pig) Write **pig** in the sentence.*

• *Read sentence 5: **It has a (blank).** What does the picture show? (grin) Write **grin** in the sentence.*

• *Now let's read all of the sentences together. Move your finger under each word as we read. Number 1: **Would you like a sip?** 2. **This is how to knit.** 3. **It has a fin.** 4. **It is a little pig.** 5. **It has a grin.***

• *Point to number 6. What do you see in the picture? (a big ship) Write a sentence about the picture. (Answers vary.) Then read your sentence to a classmate.*

Day 4

SKILLS:

**Phonics/
Word Analysis**

- Read words with common spelling patterns
- Read high-frequency and sight words
- Read regularly spelled one-syllable words

Comprehension

- Describe a picture using complete sentences

Writing

- Use developing knowledge of letter-sound correspondences to spell independently
- Print legibly and space letters and words appropriately

Writing Short *i* Word Sentences

Distribute the Day 4 activity and pencils. Say:

- *Look at the first picture. What do you see?* (a pig holding a first place ribbon) *Now look at the words in the first box. These words make up a sentence that tells about the picture. The words are out of order. Unscramble the words to write a sentence about the picture. Put your pencil down when you are finished.*

- *Look at the next picture. What do you see?* (a boy with a backpack) *Yes, this is Gabe from last week's story. He's going on a field trip. Look at the words in the box. These words make up a sentence that tells about the picture. The words are out of order. Unscramble the words to write a sentence about the picture. Put your pencil down when you are finished.*

- *Look at the words in the last box. Point to each word as we read it:* **grin**, **big**. *Write a sentence that uses the two words in the box. Then draw a picture about your sentence.* (Answers vary.)

Day 4 activity

Day 5

SKILLS:

**Phonics/
Word Analysis**

- Read words with common spelling patterns
- Use context clues in decoding words

Phonics Game

Review the short **i** word families students learned this week by playing the following game.

Materials: 4 index cards per group, labeled -**ig**, -**in**, -**ip**, and -**it**

Preparation: Divide the class into groups of four. Give each group a set of word family cards. **How to Play:** Pick a "mystery word" from the chart below and write its first letter (or blend) on the board. Have students in each group sort through their word family cards and find all the cards that can be added to that letter to form a word. For example, if you write **b** on the board, students should determine that they can form **big**, **bin**, and **bit**.

Then give students the mystery word's clue from the chart, and have each group decide what the mystery word is (e.g., "something that is not small" must be "big") and the word family card that can be used to form it (-**ig**). Ask a volunteer from each group to hold up the correct card.

Mystery Word	Clue	Mystery Word	Clue
big	something that is not small is _____	hit	you use a bat to do this to a baseball
pin	something with a sharp point	sit	you use a chair to do this
win	if you don't lose you _____	ship	something that floats in the ocean
jig	a funny dance called a _____	grip	when you hold something tightly

Home–School Connection p. 82
Spanish version available (see p. 2)

Review It

Draw a line to the correct word family.

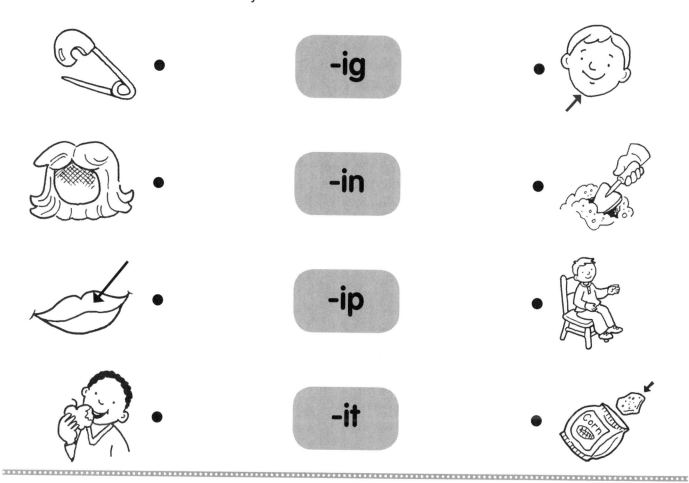

Read each word. Follow the directions.

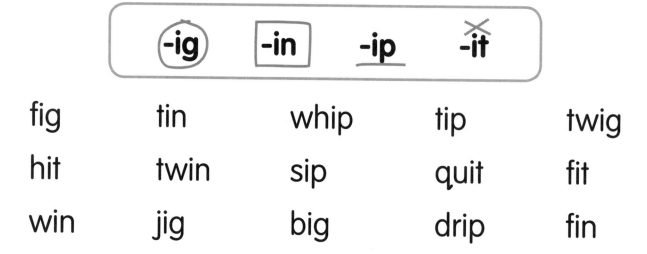

Name _____

Write It

Which word family do you hear?
Write **ig**, **in**, **ip**, or **it** to spell each word.

-ig   -in   -ip   -it

1  W _____

5  d _____

2  W _____

6  d _____

3  S _____

7  tw _____

4  S _____

8  tw _____

Read the sentences. Draw a line to the correct picture.

1 This pig is thin.

Did it win?

2 I took a chip.

I bit it.

Read It

Read the words in the box. Write the correct word to complete each sentence.

fin	ship	dig	pig	win
knit	grin	chip	sip	twin

1 Would you like a _____ ?

2 This is how to _____ .

3 It has a _____ .

4 It is a little _____ .

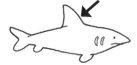

5 It has a _____ .

Write a sentence about the picture.

6 _____

Name _____

Write It

Look at the picture.
Then use the words in the box to write a sentence on the lines.

this win? Did pig

_____

_____

_____

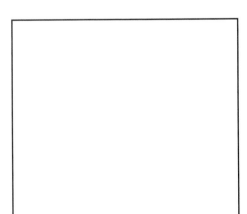

went on He a trip.

_____

_____

_____

Use the words in the box to write a sentence. Then draw a picture.

grin big

_____

_____

_____

Name _____

Short i Word Families

Write **ig**, **in**, **ip**, or **it** to finish each word.

To Parents
This week your child reviewed how to read and write words belonging to short **i** word families: **-ig**, **-in**, **-ip**, and **-it**.

 f _ _ _ _ _ _

 d _ _ _ _ _ _

 f _ _ _ _ _ _

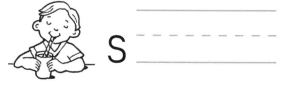 d _ _ _ _ _ _

 t w _ _ _ _ _

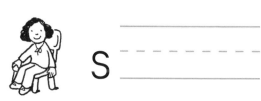 s _ _ _ _ _ _

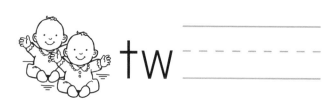 t w _ _ _ _ _

s _ _ _ _ _ _

Read the sentence. Fill in the circle below the correct picture.

| (1) | That is a nice pig. | ○ | ○ |

| (2) | It does not fit. | ○ | ○ |

| (3) | Where is my wig? | ○ | ○ |

Bob's Shop

Word Families
-ob, -op

Vocabulary
-ob: Bob, cob, job, knob, mob, rob, sob, slob
-op: chop, drop, flop, hop, mop, pop, shop, stop, top

High-Frequency Words: a, buy, can, did, he, I, is, it, like, my, on, the, they, this, to, you

Day 1

SKILLS:

Phonemic Awareness
- Generate sounds from letter patterns
- Blend two to four phonemes into recognizable words

Phonics/ Word Analysis
- Read words with common spelling patterns
- Read high-frequency and sight words
- Read regularly spelled one-syllable words

Comprehension
- Identify story characters
- Identify main idea
- Respond to who, what, where, how questions

Introducing Short *o* Word Families: *-ob, -op*

Distribute the Day 1 activity page. Point to each word ending as you say: *This week we are reading and writing two short **o** word families: /ŏb/ and /ŏp/.*

- *Point to the **-ob** box at the top of the page. Say /ŏb/. (/ŏb/) Point to the first word. Say the letter sounds with me: /b-ŏ-b/. Blend the sounds together: **Bob**. Point to the next word: /j-ŏ-b/, **job**. Point to the last word. The letter **k** is silent, so you only say the sound of **n**: /n-ŏ-b/, **knob**. What word part is the same in all of these words? (/ŏb/) Why do these words belong to the **-ob** word family?* (They all end with **ob**.)

- *Now point to the **-op** box. Say /ŏp/. (/ŏp/) Point to the first word. Say the letter sounds with me: /m-ŏ-p/, **mop**. Point to the next word: /sh-ŏ-p/, **shop**. Point to the last word: /s-t-ŏ-p/, **stop**. What word part is the same in all of these words? (/op/) These words belong to the **-op** word family.*

Listening to the Story

Say: *Listen as I read you a story that has words from the **-ob** and the **-op** word families. The title of this story is "Bob's Shop."*

Bob's job is to sell you what you need. He has a shop that is full of handy things. If you need a mop or a knob, go see Bob. If you want something to chop wood or something to pop open a can of paint, go see Bob. Bob knows how to fix most things. He is never too busy to answer questions. If you need something, just stop into Bob's shop.

Thinking About the Story

Distribute pencils. Guide students in discussing the story. Say:

- *Who is the character in this story? (Bob) What word part do you hear at the end of **Bob**, **job**, and **knob**? (/ŏb/) Which word family do those words belong to: **-ob** or **-op**? (-ob) Make a dot on **Bob**. Draw a circle around a **knob**.*

- *What was this story about? (Bob's shop) What does Bob sell besides knobs? (a mop; something to chop or pop) What word part do you hear at the end of **mop**, **chop**, and **pop**? (/ŏp/) Which word family do those words belong to? (-op) Write an X beside something that **chops**.*

Day 1 picture

SKILLS:
Phonemic Awareness
• Generate sounds from letter patterns
• Segment onset and rime

Phonics/ Word Analysis
• Read words with common spelling patterns
• Read high-frequency and sight words

Comprehension
• Recall details
• Respond to who, what, where, how questions

Writing
• Print legibly and space letters and words appropriately

Listening for *-ob* and *-op* Words

Guide a discussion that helps students recall yesterday's story. Say:

Our story was about Bob.

- *Where can someone go to get a knob?* (go see Bob; go to Bob's shop)

- *Which word family do the words **Bob** and **knob** belong to?* (-ob)

Then distribute pencils and the Day 2 activity. Say:

- *Point to the **-ob** word family at the top of the page. Let's read the **-ob** words together. Point to each word as we read: **cob, sob, job**.*

- *Now point to the **-op** word family at the top of the page. Let's read the **-op** words together. Point to each word as we read: **hop, top, stop**.*

- *Look at number 1. It shows a person doing a job. What is the first sound in **job**? (/j/) Which word part do you hear at the <u>end</u> of **job**? (/ŏb/) Write the word **job** in the boxes.*

Repeat the process for numbers 2 through 6. Then say:

- *Look at the words at the bottom of the page. Read each word. Circle the words that belong to the **-ob** word family. Underline the words that belong to the **-op** word family. Let's read the first word together: **shop**. Which word family does **shop** belong to? (-op) Draw a line under **shop**.*

Repeat the process for the remaining words.

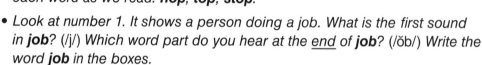

Day 2 activity

SKILLS:
Phonics/ Word Analysis
• Read words with common spelling patterns
• Read high-frequency and sight words
• Read regularly spelled one-syllable words

Comprehension
• Recall details
• Respond to who, what, where, how questions

Writing
• Print legibly and space letters and words appropriately

Writing *-ob* and *-op* Sentences

Reread the Day 1 story. Then guide a discussion about the story by saying:

Our story was about Bob's shop. What did Bob sell? (a knob; a mop; something to chop, or pop open a can of paint) *Which word family do the words **mop, chop,** and **pop** belong to?* (-op)

Distribute pencils and the Day 3 activity. Say:

*We are going to read, trace, and then write sentences that have **-ob** and **-op** words.*

- *Point to the first sentence. Move your finger under each word as we read together: **This is Bob's job**. Which words are from the **-ob** word family?* (Bob, job) *Now trace the sentence, then write the sentence again on the line below. Put your pencil down when you are finished.*

- *Point to the next sentence. Let's read it together: **He sells a knob**. Which word is from the **-ob** word family?* (knob) *Trace the sentence, then write the sentence again on the line below. Put your pencil down when you are finished.*

After students complete sentence 2, have them read sentences 1 and 2 aloud. Repeat the process for sentences 3 and 4.

Day 3 activity

Day 4

SKILLS:
**Phonics/
Word Analysis**
• Read words with
common spelling
patterns
• Read high-frequency
and sight words
• Read regularly
spelled one-syllable
words
Comprehension
• Recall details
• Respond to who,
what, where, how
questions
Writing
• Print legibly and
space letters and
words appropriately

Reading -*ob* and -*op* Words

Reread the Day 1 story if necessary. Then guide
a discussion about the story by saying:

Our story was about a place full of handy things.

• *Who had a job there?* (Bob) *What word family is
that name from?* (-ob)

• *What kind of place was it?* (a shop) *What word
family is **shop** from?* (-op)

Distribute pencils and the Day 4 activity. Say:

Listen carefully and follow my directions.

• *Put your finger on the first sentence at the top of
the page. Move your finger under each word as
we read it together: **I like it on the cob**. Underline
the word from the **-ob** word family. (cob) Draw a
line to the picture that matches the sentence.*

Repeat the process for numbers 2 through 4. Then point to the word box
at the bottom of the page and say:

• *Point to this word box. Let's read the words together: **shop**, **mop**, **stop**. Each
sentence below is missing one word. Look at the picture next to each sentence.
Write one of the words from the word box to complete each sentence.*

Day 4 activity

Day 5

SKILLS:
**Phonemic
Awareness**
• Recognize a new
spoken word when a
phoneme is added,
changed, or removed
**Phonics/
Word Analysis**
• Read words with
common spelling
patterns

Oral Language Activity

Reinforce this week's word families by using a phoneme substitution activity.
Introduce and model the call-and-response below.

All: *Let's make a word family; we'll have fun.*
All: *Let's make a word family; **-ob** is one.*

Students: *What's the word?*
Teacher: *The word is **job**.*
Students: *What do we change?*
Teacher: *Change /j/ to /k/.*
Students: ***Cob!***
Teacher: ***Cob** is the word.*

Students: *What's the word?*
Teacher: *The word is **cob**.*
Students: *What do we change?*
Teacher: *Change /k/ to /r/.*
Students: ***Rob!***
Teacher: ***Rob** is the word.*

Continue the chant using **Bob, knob, mob, slob.**

Then repeat the chant using **-op** family words: /t/ top, /h/ hop, /p/ pop,
/sl/ slop, /dr/ drop, /ch/ chop, /sh/ shop, etc.

Extension: Write **-ob** and **-op** words on index cards. Recite the chant above
using letter names instead of sounds. For example, say: *Change **c** to **r**.* After
students say the new word, hold up the corresponding word card (**rob**) as
you say the word.

**Home–School
Connection p. 90**
Spanish version
available (see p. 2)

Bob's Shop

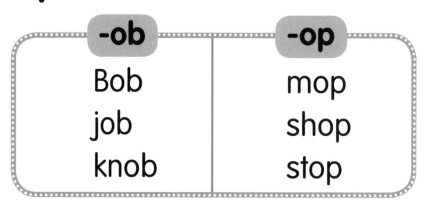

-ob	**-op**
Bob	mop
job	shop
knob	stop

Name ________________________________

Bob's Shop

-ob	**-op**
cob	hop
sob	top
job	stop

Write the correct word in the boxes.

1 

2 

3 

4 

5 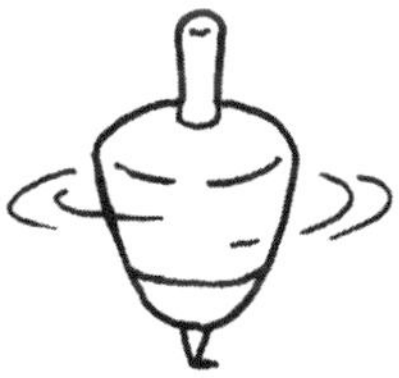

6 

Circle the **-ob** words. Underline the **-op** words.

-ob **-op**

shop	Bob	top	pop	mob	drop
mop	knob	cob	rob	flop	slob

Name _____

Bob's Shop

Read the sentence. Trace the sentence. Then write the sentence on the line below.

1 This is Bob's job.

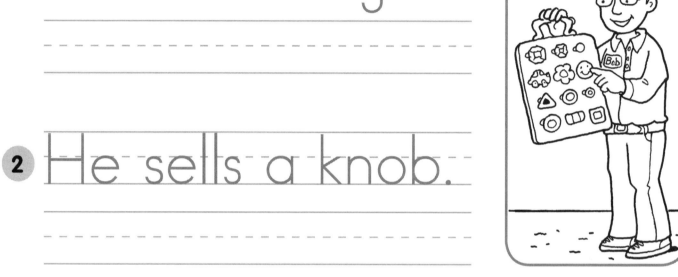

2 He sells a knob.

3 Visit Bob's shop.

4 Buy a mop.

Everyday Literacy: Reading and Writing • EMC 2419 • © Evan-Moor Corp.

Name _____

Bob's Shop

Read the sentence. Draw a line to the correct picture.

1 I like it on the cob.

2 I like my job.

3 I like to hop.

4 Did they drop?

Write the correct word to complete each sentence.

> **shop** **mop** **stop**

1 Can you _____ ?

2 Can you _____ ?

3 Can you _____ ?

Name _____

Bob's Shop

What to Do
Read the story with your child and look at the picture together.
Then have your child circle words in the story that end with **-ob**
and draw a line under words that end with **-op**.

To Parents
This week your child learned to read and write words from the **-ob** and **-op** word families.

Bob has a job. He works in a shop.
Do you want a knob? Do you want a mop?
Stop in at Bob's shop. Go see Bob!

What to Do Next
Ask your child to draw a picture of a job that he or she would like to do on a sheet of paper.

-og
-ot

Dog Meets Frog

Word Families

-og, -ot

Vocabulary

-og: clog, dog, fog, hog, jog, log, frog, smog
-ot: cot, Dot, got, hot, knot, lot, not, pot, spot, tot, trot

High-Frequency Words: a, can, for, has, I, is, it, my, off, on, or, over, ran, went

Day 1

SKILLS:

Phonemic Awareness

• Generate sounds from letter patterns

• Blend two to four phonemes into recognizable words

Phonics/ Word Analysis

• Read words with common spelling patterns

• Read high-frequency and sight words

• Read regularly spelled one-syllable words

Comprehension

• Identify story characters

• Identify main idea

• Respond to who, what, where, how questions

Introducing Short *o* Word Families: *-og, -ot*

Distribute the Day 1 activity page. Point to each word ending as you say: *This week we are reading and writing two more short **o** word families: /ŏg/ and /ŏt/.*

- *Point to the **-og** box at the top of the page. Say /ŏg/. (/ŏg/) Point to the first word. Say the letter sounds with me: /d-ŏ-g/. Blend the sounds together: **dog**. Point to the next word: /j-ŏ-g/, **jog**. Point to the last word: /f-ŏ-g/, **fog**. What word part is the same in all of these words? (/ŏg/) These words belong to the **-og** word family.*

- *Now point to the **-ot** box. Say /ŏt/. (/ŏt/) Point to the first word. Say the letter sounds with me: /d-ŏ-t/, **dot**. Point to the next word: /s-p-ŏ-t/, **spot**. Point to the last word: /t-r-ŏ-t/, **trot**. What word part is the same in all of these words? (/ŏt/) These words belong to the **-ot** word family.*

Listening to the Story

Say: *Listen as I read you a story that has words from the **-og** and the **-ot** word families. The title of this story is "Dog Meets Frog."*

My dog Dot is friendly. I like to take her with me when I jog. She trots along and wags her tail. We jog in rain, sun, or fog. One day, we jogged by a log. On it sat a frog. Dot wagged her tail and sniffed the frog. All of a sudden, the frog said "Croak!" and jumped off its spot on the log. I guess I should have known a frog wouldn't want to be sniffed by a dog. Next time we'll know not to bother a frog on a log.

Thinking About the Story

Distribute pencils. Guide students in discussing the story. Say:

- *Who are the characters in this story? (a boy, a dog, a frog) What word part do you hear at the end of **dog**, **frog**, **log**? (/ŏg/) Which word family do those words belong to: **-ot** or **-og**? (-og) Make a dot on the **dog**, the **frog**, and the **log**.*

- *What was this story about? (when Dot saw a frog) What scared the frog? (Dot sniffed it.) What word part do you hear at the end of **Dot**? (/ŏt/) Which word family does that word belong to? (-ot) Write an **X** beside the animal that can **trot**.*

Day 1 picture

Day 2

SKILLS:

Phonemic Awareness
- Generate sounds from letter patterns
- Segment onset and rimes

Phonics/ Word Analysis
- Read words with common spelling patterns
- Read high-frequency and sight words
- Read regularly spelled one-syllable words

Comprehension
- Recall details
- Respond to who, what, where, how questions

Writing
- Print legibly and space letters and words appropriately

Listening for *-og* and *-ot* Words

Guide a discussion that helps students recall yesterday's story. Say:

*Our story was about a boy and his dog. What did the dog scare away? (a frog on a log) Which word family do the words **frog** and **log** belong to? (-og)*

Then distribute pencils and the Day 2 activity. Say:

- *Point to the **-og** word family at the top of the page. Let's read the **-og** words together. Point to each word as we read: **hog**, **log**, **frog**.*

- *Now point to the **-ot** word family at the top of the page. Let's read the **-ot** words together. Point to each word as we read: **pot**, **cot**, **hot**.*

- *Look at number 1. It shows a hog. What is the first sound in **hog**? (/h/) Which word part do you hear at the <u>end</u> of **hog**? (/ŏg/) Write the word **hog** in the boxes.*

Repeat the process for numbers 2 through 6. Then say:

- *Look at the words at the bottom of the page. Read each word. Circle the words that belong to the **-og** word family. Underline the words that belong to the **-ot** word family. Let's read the first word together: **fog**. Which word family does **fog** belong to? (-og) Circle the word **fog**.*

Repeat the process for the remaining words.

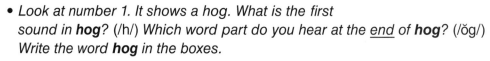

Day 2 activity

Day 3

SKILLS:

Phonics/ Word Analysis
- Read words with common spelling patterns
- Read high-frequency and sight words
- Read regularly spelled one-syllable words

Comprehension
- Recall details
- Respond to who, what, where, how questions

Writing
- Print legibly and space letters and words appropriately

Writing *-og* and *-ot* Sentences

Reread the Day 1 story. Then guide a discussion about the story by saying:

Our story was about a dog who got too close to a frog. What was the dog's name? (Dot)

- *What happened when Dot sniffed the frog? (It croaked and jumped off its spot on the log.) Which word family do the words **Dot** and **spot** belong to? (-ot)*

Distribute pencils and the Day 3 activity. Say:

*We are going to read, trace, and then write sentences that have **-og** and **-ot** words.*

- *Point to the first sentence. Move your finger under each word as we read together: **My dog is Dot**. Which word is from the **-ot** word family? (Dot) Now trace the sentence, then write the sentence again on the line below. Put your pencil down when you are finished.*

- *Point to the next sentence. Let's read it together: **Dot can trot**. Which words are from the **-ot** word family? (Dot, trot) Trace the sentence, then write the sentence again on the line below. Put your pencil down when you are finished.*

After students complete sentence 2, have them read sentences 1 and 2 aloud. Repeat the process for sentences 3 and 4.

Day 3 activity

SKILLS:

Phonics/ Word Analysis
- Read words with common spelling patterns
- Read high-frequency and sight words

Comprehension
- Recall details
- Respond to who, what, where, how questions

Writing
- Print legibly and space letters and words appropriately

Reading *-og* and *-ot* Words

Reread the Day 1 story if necessary. Then guide a discussion about the story by saying:

*There was a dog in our story. What animal did the dog meet? (frog) What word family does **frog** belong to? (-og)*

Distribute pencils and the Day 4 activity. Say:

Listen carefully and follow my directions.

- *Put your finger on the first sentence at the top of the page. Move your finger under each word as we read it together: **I went for a jog**. Underline the word from the **-og** word family. (jog) Draw a line to the picture that matches the sentence.*

Repeat the process for numbers 2 through 4. Then point to the word box at the bottom of the page and say:

- *Point to this word box. Let's read the words together: **knot**, **clog**, **spot**. Each sentence below is missing one word. Look at the picture next to each sentence. Write one of the words from the word box to complete each sentence.*

Day 4 activity

SKILLS:

Phonemic Awareness
- Recognize a new spoken word when a phoneme is added, changed, or removed

Phonics/ Word Analysis
- Read words with common spelling patterns

Home–School Connection p. 98
Spanish version available (see p. 2)

Oral Language Activity

Reinforce this week's word families by using a phoneme substitution activity. Introduce and model the call-and-response below.

All: *Let's make a word family; we'll have fun.*
All: *Let's make a word family; **-og** is one.*

Students: *What's the word?*
Teacher: *The word is **jog**.*
Students: *What do we change?*
Teacher: *Change /j/ to /f/.*
Students: ***Fog!***
Teacher: ***Fog** is the word.*

Students: *What's the word?*
Teacher: *The word is **fog**.*
Students: *What do we change?*
Teacher: *Change /f/ to /d/.*
Students: ***Dog!***
Teacher: ***Dog** is the word.*

Continue the chant using ***frog**, **log**, **smog**, **hog**.*

Then repeat the chant using **-ot** family words: */n/ not, /h/ hot, /p/ pot, /l/ lot, /g/ got, /d/ dot,* etc.

Extension: Write **-og** and **-ot** words on index cards. Recite the chant above using letter names instead of sounds. For example, say: *Change **f** to **d**.* After students say the new word, hold up the corresponding word card (**dog**) as you say the word.

Name _____

Dog Meets Frog

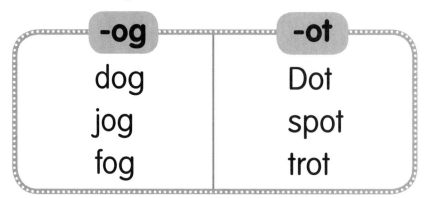

-og	**-ot**
dog	Dot
jog	spot
fog	trot

Name _____

Dog Meets Frog

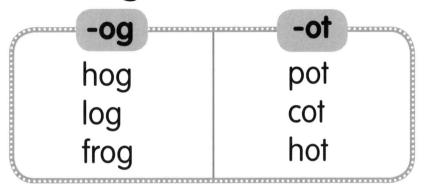

-og	**-ot**
hog	pot
log	cot
frog	hot

Write the correct word in the boxes.

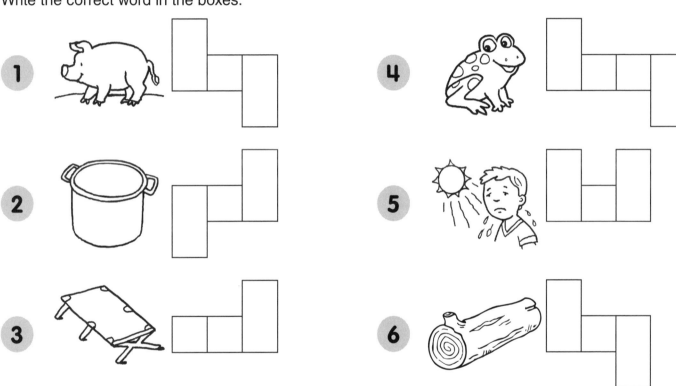

Circle the **-og** words. Underline the **-ot** words.

-og	**-ot**

fog	dot	tot	got	dog	jog
spot	clog	not	frog	lot	smog

Name _____

Dog Meets Frog

Read the sentence. Trace the sentence. Then write the sentence on the line below.

1 My dog is Dot.

2 Dot can trot.

3 Frog is on a log.

4 Frog is off a log.

Everyday Literacy: Reading and Writing • EMC 2419 • © Evan-Moor Corp.

Name _____

Dog Meets Frog

Read the sentence. Draw a line to the correct picture.

1 I went for a jog.

2 I ran over a log.

3 Is it fog or smog?

4 Is it a hog or a frog?

Write the correct word to complete each sentence.

knot   clog   spot

1 It has a _____.

2 It has a _____.

3 It has a _____.

Name _____

Dog Meets Frog

What to Do
Read the story with your child and look at the picture together. Then have your child circle words in the story that end with **-og** and draw a line under words that end with **-ot**.

To Parents
This week your child learned to read and write words from the **-og** and **-ot** word families.

Dot and I jog. We jog in rain, sun, or fog. We saw a log. On it sat a frog. Dot sniffed the frog. Croak! The frog got off the log!

What to Do Next
Work together with your child to write a story using words from the **-og** and **-ot** word families.

Everyday Literacy: Reading and Writing • EMC 2419 • © Evan-Moor Corp.

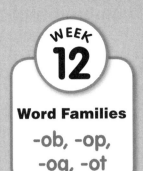

Review It

Short *o* Word Family Words:
-ob: Bob, cob, job, knob, rob, sob
-op: drop, hop, mop, pop, shop, stop, top
-og: clog, dog, fog, frog, jog, log, smog
-ot: cot, dot, got, hot, knot, lot, not, pot, spot, tot
High-Frequency Words: a, am, at, does, have, he, here, I, is, it, little, my, not, on, sit, that, the, was, went, why

---

Day 1

SKILLS:

Phonemic Awareness
• Generate sounds from letter patterns
• Blend two to four phonemes into recognizable words

Phonics/Word Analysis
• Read words with common spelling patterns
• Read regularly spelled one-syllable words

Listening for Short *o* Word Families

Distribute the Day 1 activity and a pencil to each student. Then say:

• *Let's review the short **o** word families we learned during the past few weeks. Point to each gray box as we read each word family ending together: **-ob**, **-op**, **-og**, **-ot**. Now we'll match each picture to its word family. Point to the top. Say **top**. (top) What word family does **top** belong to? (-op) What letters stand for /ŏp/? (op) Draw a line from the top to the correct word family.*

• *Point to the cot. Say **cot**. (cot) What word family does **cot** belong to? (-ot) What letters stand for /ŏt/? (ot) Draw a line from the cot to the correct word family.*

• *Point to the cob. Say **cob**. (cob) What word family does **cob** belong to? (-ob) What letters stand for /ŏb/? (ob) Draw a line from the cob to the correct word family.*

Repeat the process for the remaining picture words: **dog**, **sob**, **smog**, **stop**, and **pot**.

Discriminating *-ob, -op, -og, -ot*

Direct students' attention to the bottom half of the page. Then say:

• *These words belong to short **o** word families. We're going to read each word and follow the directions shown in the box. Let's start with the **-ob** word family. When you read a word that belongs to the **-ob** family, draw a circle around it. Do that now. (pause) Which words did you circle? (rob, Bob, knob)*

• *Now look for words from the **-op** word family. When you read a word that belongs to the **-op** family, draw a box around it. Do that now. (pause) Which words did you box? (top, shop, drop, mop, pop)*

• *Now look for words from the **-ot** word family. When you read a word that belongs to the **-ot** family, draw a line under it. Do that now. (pause) Which words did you underline? (not, spot, dot, got)*

• *Now look for words from the **-og** word family. When you read a word that belongs to the **-og** family, write an **X** above it. Do that now. (pause) Which words did you mark with an **X**? (fog, clog, frog)*

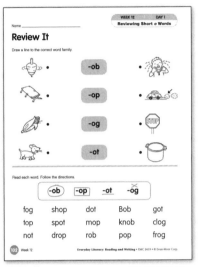

Day 1 activity

SKILLS:

Phonemic Awareness

• Segment onset and rime

Phonics/ Word Analysis

• Read words with common spelling patterns

• Read high-frequency and sight words

• Read regularly spelled one-syllable words

Writing

• Print legibly and space letters and words appropriately

Writing Short *o* Word Family Words

Distribute the Day 2 activity and a pencil to each student. Then say:

• *Look at the word endings in the box. Let's read them together: **-ob, -op, -og, -ot**. Now look at the pictures below.*

• *Point to picture number 1. It shows a dog. Which word family does **dog** belong to? (-og) Write the missing letters to finish the word **dog**.*

• *Point to picture number 2. It shows a dot. Which word family does **dot** belong to? (-ot) Write the missing letters to finish the word **dot**.*

Repeat the process for the remaining words: **cob, cot, job, jog, knob, knot**. Then say:

• *Now we're going to read sentences and draw a line to the matching picture. Point to number 1. Let's read together: **I have a cob. It is hot**. Draw a line to the picture that matches the sentences.*

Repeat the process for the remaining sentences.

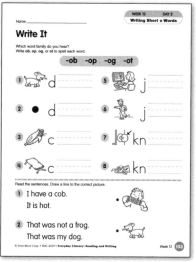

Day 2 activity

SKILLS:

Phonics/ Word Analysis

• Read words with common spelling patterns

• Read regularly spelled one-syllable words

Writing

• Use developing knowledge of letter-sound correspondences to spell independently

• Print legibly and space letters and words appropriately

Reading Words with *-ob, -op, -og, -ot*

Distribute the Day 3 activity and a pencil to each student. Say:

• *The words in the box belong to short **o** word families. Point to each word and read with me: **sob, cot, frog, tot, fog, shop, hot, top, log, hop**.*

• *Point to sentence number 1. Move your finger under each word as we read together: **Here is Bob's (blank)**. What does the picture show? (shop) Write **shop** to complete the sentence. Use the word box if you need help.*

• *Read sentence 2: **Sit on the (blank)**. What does the picture show? (log) Write **log** in the sentence.*

• *Read sentence 3: **I am (blank)**. What does the picture show? (hot) Write **hot** in the sentence.*

• *Read sentence 4: **He is a little (blank)**. What does the picture show? (tot) Write **tot** in the sentence.*

• *Read sentence 5: **Why does he (blank)?** What does the picture show? (sob) Write **sob** in the sentence.*

• *Point to number 6. What do you see in the picture? (frog) Write a sentence about the picture. (Answers vary.) Then read your sentence to a classmate.*

Day 3 activity

Day 4

SKILLS:

Phonics/ Word Analysis
• Read words with common spelling patterns
• Read high-frequency and sight words
• Read regularly spelled one-syllable words

Comprehension
• Describe a picture using complete sentences

Writing
• Use developing knowledge of letter-sound correspondences to spell independently
• Print legibly and space letters and words appropriately

Writing Short *o* Word Sentences

Distribute the Day 4 activity and pencils. Say:

- *Look at the first picture. What do you see?* (Bob in his shop) *Now look at the words in the first box. These words make up a sentence that tells about the picture. The words are out of order. Unscramble the words to write a sentence about the picture. Put your pencil down when you are finished.*

- *Look at the next picture. What do you see?* (a frog on a log) *Now look at the words in the box. These words make up a sentence that tells about the picture. The words are out of order. Unscramble the words to write a sentence about the picture. Put your pencil down when you are finished.*

- *Look at the words in the last box. Point to each word as we read it:* **spot**, **dog**. *Write a sentence that uses these words. Then draw a picture about your sentence.* (Answers vary.)

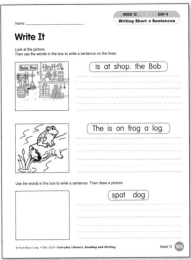

Day 4 activity

Day 5

SKILLS:

Phonics/ Word Analysis
• Read words with common spelling patterns
• Use context clues in decoding words

Phonics Game

Review the short **o** word families students learned this week by playing the following game.

Materials: 4 index cards per group, labeled **-ob**, **-op**, **-og**, and **-ot**

Preparation: Divide the class into groups of four. Give each group a set of word family cards.

How to Play: Pick a "mystery word" from the chart below and write its first letter (or blend) on the board. Have students in each group sort through their word family cards and find all the cards that can be added to that letter to form a word. For example, if you write **c** on the board, students should determine that they can form **cob**, **cop**, and **cot**.

Then give students the mystery word's clue from the chart, and have each group decide what the mystery word is (e.g., "another name for a police officer" must be "cop") and the word family card that can be used to form it (**-op**). Ask a volunteer from each group to hold up the correct card.

Mystery Word	Clue	Mystery Word	Clue
cop	another name for a police officer	**dot**	a small black mark
gob	you might find a _____ of gum on your shoe	**jog**	to run slowly
lot	a place where cars park	**mop**	something you use to clean the floor
pop	corn does this when it's heated	**knot**	sometimes your shoelace gets into a _____

Home–School Connection p. 106
Spanish version available (see p. 2)

Name _____

Review It

Draw a line to the correct word family.

 •

-ob

 •

-op

 •

-og

 •

-ot

Read each word. Follow the directions.

(-ob)   [-op]   <u>-ot</u>   ✗-og

fog	shop	dot	Bob	got
top	spot	mop	knob	clog
not	drop	rob	pop	frog

Name _____

Write It

Which word family do you hear?
Write **ob**, **op**, **og**, or **ot** to spell each word.

-ob   -op   -og   -ot

1  d _____

2 ● d _____

3 c _____

4 c _____

5 j _____

6 j _____

7 kn _____

8 kn _____

Read the sentences. Draw a line to the correct picture.

1 I have a cob.
   It is hot.

2 That was not a frog.
   That was my dog.

Name _____

Read It

Read the words in the box. Write the correct word to complete each sentence.

sob	cot	frog	tot	fog
shop	hot	top	log	hop

1 Here is Bob's _____ .

2 Sit on the _____ .

3 I am _____ .

4 He is a little _____ .

5 Why does he _____ ?

Write a sentence about the picture.

6 _____

Name _____

Write It

Look at the picture.
Then use the words in the box to write a sentence on the lines.

is at shop. the Bob

_____
_____
_____

The is on frog a log.

_____
_____
_____

Use the words in the box to write a sentence. Then draw a picture.

spot   dog

_____
_____
_____

Name _____

Short o Word Families

WEEK 12

Home–School Connection

To Parents
This week your child reviewed how to read and write words belonging to short **o** word families: **-ob**, **-op**, **-og**, and **-ot**.

Write **ob**, **op**, **og**, or **ot** to finish each word.

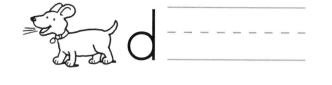 d _____

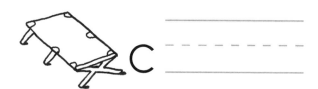 d _____

 c _____

 c _____

 j _____

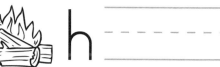 j _____

 h _____

 h _____

Read the sentence. Fill in the circle below the correct picture.

1 That is a lot.
○   ○

2 It went pop!
○   ○

3 Is it a dog?
○   ●

Fun in a Tub

Word Families
-ub, -ug
Vocabulary
-ub: cub, club, flub, hub, rub, scrub, stub, sub, tub
-ug: bug, chug, glug, hug, jug, mug, plug, rug, shrug, slug, snug, tug
High-Frequency Words: a, and, can, get, give, goes, here, I, in, is, it, on, see, the, where, you

Day 1

SKILLS:
Phonemic Awareness
- Generate sounds from letter patterns
- Blend two to four phonemes into recognizable words

Phonics/ Word Analysis
- Read words with common spelling patterns
- Read high-frequency and sight words
- Read regularly spelled one-syllable words

Comprehension
- Identify story characters
- Identify main idea
- Respond to who, what, where, how questions

Introducing Short *u* Word Families: *-ub, -ug*

Distribute the Day 1 activity page. Point to each word ending as you say: *This week we are reading and writing two short **u** word families: /ŭb/ and /ŭg/.*

- *Point to the **-ub** box at the top of the page. Say /ŭb/. (/ŭb/) Point to the first word. Say the letter sounds with me: /k-ŭ-b/. Blend the sounds together: **cub**. Point to the next word: /t-ŭ-b/, **tub**. Point to the last word: /k-l-ŭ-b/, **club**. What word part is the same in all of these words? (/ŭb/) These words belong to the **-ub** word family.*

- *Now point to the **-ug** box. Say /ŭg/. (/ŭg/) Point to the first word. Say the letter sounds with me: /b-ŭ-g/, **bug**. Point to the next word: /t-ŭ-g/, **tug**. Point to the last word: /p-l-ŭ-g/, **plug**. What word part is the same in all of these words? (/ŭg/) These words belong to the **-ug** word family.*

Listening to the Story

Say: *Listen as I read you a story that has words from the **-ub** and the **-ug** word families. The title of this story is "Fun in a Tub."*

Colton loves to take a bath. He brings his toy cub and sets him on the tub. Colton pretends to be a sub. Then, he pretends his fingers are a water bug. After that, Colton starts to scrub and rub. When he's done, he tugs on the plug. He likes to hear the water gurgle down the drain—glug, glug, glug. Colton is a member of the Fun in the Tub Club!

Thinking About the Story

Distribute pencils. Guide students in discussing the story. Say:

- *Who is the character in this story?* (Colton) *What is the setting?* (a tub) *What word part do you hear at the end of **cub** and **tub**?* (/ŭb/) *Which word family does the word **cub** belong to: **-ub** or **-ug**?* (-ub) *Make a dot on the **cub**.*

- *What was this story about?* (having fun in the tub) *What does Colton pretend to be?* (a bug or a sub) *What word part do you hear at the end of **bug**, **tug**, and **plug**?* (/ŭg/) *Which word family do those words belong to?* (-ug)

Day 1 picture

SKILLS:

Phonemic Awareness

- Generate sounds from letter patterns
- Segment onset and rime

Phonics/ Word Analysis

- Read words with common spelling patterns
- Read high-frequency and sight words
- Read regularly spelled one-syllable words

Comprehension

- Recall details
- Respond to who, what, where, how questions

Writing

- Print legibly and space letters and words appropriately

Learning More *-ub* and *-ug* Words

Guide a discussion that helps students recall yesterday's story. Say:

Our story was about tub time for Colton. What did Colton do besides play in the tub? (scrub, rub) *Which word family do those words belong to?* (-ub)

Then distribute pencils and the Day 2 activity. Say:

- *Point to the **-ub** word family at the top of the page. Let's read the **-ub** words together. Point to each word as we read:* **sub, club, tub**.

- *Now point to the **-ug** word family at the top of the page. Let's read the **-ug** words together. Point to each word as we read:* **rug, jug, plug**.

- *Look at number 1. It shows a jug. What is the first sound in **jug**?* (/j/) *Which word part do you hear at the <u>end</u> of **jug**?* (/ŭg/) *Write the word **jug** in the boxes.*

Repeat the process for numbers 2 through 6. Then say:

- *Look at the words at the bottom of the page. Read each word. Circle the words that belong to the **-ub** word family. Underline the words that belong to the **-ug** word family. Let's read the first word together:* **rub**. *Which word family does **rub** belong to?* (-ub) *Circle the word **rub**.*

Repeat the process for the remaining words.

Day 2 activity

SKILLS:

Phonics/ Word Study

- Read words with common spelling patterns
- Read high-frequency and sight words
- Read regularly spelled one-syllable words

Comprehension

- Recall details
- Respond to who, what, where, how questions

Writing

- Print legibly and space letters and words appropriately

Writing *-ub* and *-ug* Sentences

Reread the Day 1 story. Then guide a discussion about the story by saying:

Our story was about bath time for Colton.

- *What does the water do when he tugs on the plug?* (goes glug, glug)

- *Which word family do the words **tug**, **plug**, and **glug** belong to?* (-ug)

Distribute pencils and the Day 3 activity. Say:

*We are going to read, trace, and then write sentences that have **-ub** and **-ug** words.*

- *Point to the first sentence. Move your finger under each word as we read together:* **I get in the tub**. *Which word is from the **-ub** word family?* (tub) *Now trace the sentence, then write the sentence again on the line below. Put your pencil down when you are finished.*

- *Point to the next sentence. Let's read it together:* **I scrub and rub**. *Which words are from the **-ub** word family?* (scrub, rub) *Trace the sentence, then write the sentence again on the line below. Put your pencil down when you are finished.*

After students complete sentence 2, have them read sentences 1 and 2 aloud. Repeat the process for sentences 3 and 4.

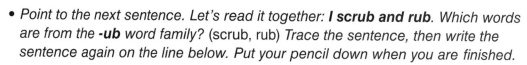

Day 3 activity

Day 4

SKILLS:

**Phonics/
Word Analysis**

- Read words with common spelling patterns
- Read high-frequency and sight words
- Read regularly spelled one-syllable words

Comprehension

- Recall details
- Respond to who, what, where, how questions

Writing

- Print legibly and space letters and words appropriately

Reading *-ub* and *-ug* Words

Reread the Day 1 story if necessary. Then guide a discussion about the story by saying:

Our story was about a boy named Colton.

- *Where did he have fun? (in the tub) What word family is the word **tub** from? (-ub)*

- *What did he tug when he was done? (plug) What word family are **tug** and **plug** from? (-ug)*

Distribute pencils and the Day 4 activity. Say:

Listen carefully and follow my directions.

- *Put your finger on the first sentence at the top of the page. Move your finger under each word as we read it together: **Where is a slug?** Underline the word from the **-ug** word family. (slug) Draw a line to the picture that matches the sentence.*

Repeat the process for numbers 2 through 4. Then point to the word box at the bottom of the page and say:

- *Point to this word box. Let's read the words together: **bug**, **hug**, **scrub**. Each sentence below is missing one word. Look at the picture next to each sentence. Write one of the words from the word box to complete each sentence.*

Day 4 activity

Day 5

SKILLS:

**Phonemic
Awareness**

- Recognize a new spoken word when a phoneme is added, changed, or removed

**Phonics/
Word Analysis**

- Read words with common spelling patterns

Oral Language Activity

Reinforce this week's word families by using a phoneme substitution activity. Introduce and model the call-and-response below.

All: *Let's make a word family; we'll have fun.*
All: *Let's make a word family; **-ub** is one.*

Students: *What's the word?*
Teacher: *The word is **cub**.*
Students: *What do we change?*
Teacher: *Change /k/ to /r/.*
Students: ***Rub!***
Teacher: ***Rub** is the word.*

Students: *What's the word?*
Teacher: *The word is **rub**.*
Students: *What do we change?*
Teacher: *Change /r/ to /t/.*
Students: ***Tub!***
Teacher: ***Tub** is the word.*

Continue the chant using: **hub, scrub, dub, nub.**

Then repeat the chant using **-ug** family words: /h/ hug, /b/ bug, /r/ rug, /p/ pug, /t/ tug, /pl/ plug, etc.

Extension: Write **-ub** and **-ug** words on index cards. Recite the chant above using letter names instead of sounds. For example, say: *Change **r** to **t**.* After students say the new word, hold up the corresponding word card (**tub**) as you say the word.

Home–School Connection p. 114
Spanish version available (see p. 2)

Name _____

Fun in a Tub

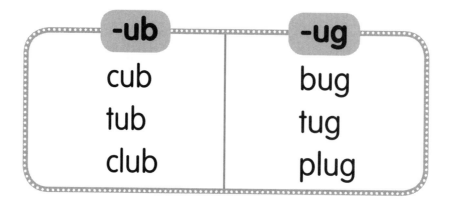

-ub	-ug
cub	bug
tub	tug
club	plug

Everyday Literacy: Reading and Writing • EMC 2419 • © Evan-Moor Corp.

Name _____

Fun in a Tub

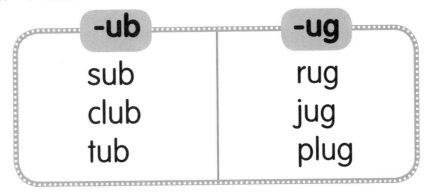

-ub	-ug
sub	rug
club	jug
tub	plug

Write the correct word in the boxes.

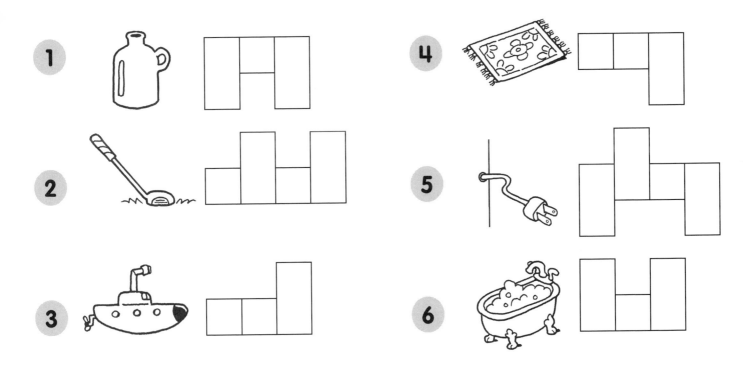

1

2

3

4

5

6

Circle the **-ub** words. Underline the **-ug** words.

(-ub)   -ug

rub	tug	cub	mug	hug	flub
snug	bug	chug	scrub	hub	stub

Name _____

Fun in a Tub

Read the sentence. Trace the sentence. Then write the sentence on the line below.

1 I get in the tub.

2 I scrub and rub.

3 Tug on the plug.

4 It goes glug.

Everyday Literacy: Reading and Writing • EMC 2419 • © Evan-Moor Corp.

Fun in a Tub

Read the sentence. Draw a line to the correct picture.

1 Where is a slug?

2 Where is a mug?

3 Here is a cub.

4 Here is a shrub.

Write the correct word to complete each sentence.

bug   hug   scrub

1 Can you see a _____?

2 Can you _____?

3 Can you give a _____?

Name _____

Fun in a Tub

What to Do
Read the story with your child and look at the picture together.
Then have your child circle words in the story that end with **-ub**
and draw a line under words that end with **-ug**.

WEEK 13

Home–School Connection

To Parents
This week your child learned to read and write words from the **-ub** and **-ug** word families.

See Colton in the tub. He can be a sub.

He can be a water bug. See him scrub and rub!

Now he tugs on the plug. The water goes glug!

What to Do Next
Work together with your child to write a story using words from the **-ub** and **-ug** word families.

WEEK 14

-um
-unk

Out Goes the Junk

Word Families: -um, -unk

Vocabulary
-um: chum, drum, glum, gum, hum, mum, plum, strum, sum
-unk: bunk, chunk, dunk, flunk, hunk, junk, plunk, skunk, sunk, trunk

High-Frequency Words: a, are, ate, can, do, eat, have, he, here, I, my, in, is, it, she, some, think, toys, want, you

---

Day 1

SKILLS:

Phonemic Awareness
• Generate sounds from letter patterns
• Blend two to four phonemes into recognizable words

Phonics/ Word Analysis
• Read words with common spelling patterns
• Read high-frequency and sight words
• Read regularly spelled one-syllable words

Comprehension
• Identify story characters
• Identify main idea
• Respond to who, what, where, how questions

Introducing Short *u* Word Families: *-um, -unk*

Distribute the Day 1 activity page. Point to each word ending as you say: *This week we are reading and writing two more short **u** word families: **/ŭm/** and **/ŭnk/**.*

• *Point to the **-um** box at the top of the page. Say **/ŭm/**. (/ŭm/) Point to the first word. Say the letter sounds with me: **/g-ŭ-m/**. Blend the sounds together: **gum**. Point to the next word: **/h-ŭ-m/**, **hum**. Point to the last word: **/d-r-ŭ-m/**, **drum**. What word part is the same in all of these words? (/ŭm/) These words belong to the **-um** word family.*

• *Now point to the **-unk** box. Say **/ŭnk/**. (/ŭnk/) Point to the first word. Say the letter sounds with me: **/b-ŭ-n-k/**, **bunk**. Point to the next word: **/j-ŭ-n-k/**, **junk**. Point to the last word: **/s-k-ŭ-n-k/**, **skunk**. What word part is the same in all of these words? (-unk) These words belong to the **-unk** word family.*

Listening to the Story

Say: *Listen as I read you a story that has words from the **-um** and the **-unk** word families. The title of this story is "Out Goes the Junk."*

I knew if Mom saw our room, she would be very glum. We'd flunk her clean-room test! So, my little brother and I made up our bunk beds. Then we put most of our toys into the trunk, all except my brother's toy skunk. I let him keep that on his bed. While we were cleaning, we found some awful junk—a plum pit, a chunk of old wood, gum wrappers, and a broken oatmeal-box drum. Plunk! Into the trash can they went. Now when Mom comes in, we're ready for inspection!

Thinking About the Story

Distribute pencils. Guide students in discussing the story. Say:

• *Who are the characters? (two brothers) Where did they put their toys? (trunk) What word part do you hear at the end of **trunk** and **junk**? (/ŭnk/) Which word family do they belong to: **-unk** or **-um**? (-unk) Make a dot on the **trunk**.*

• *What was this story about? (brothers cleaning their room) What was the oatmeal box? (drum) What word part do you hear at the end of **drum**? (/ŭm/) Which word family does it belong to? (-um) Write an **X** to show where they put the broken **drum**.*

Day 1 picture

Day 2

SKILLS:

Phonemic Awareness

- Generate sounds from letter patterns
- Segment onset and rime

Phonics/ Word Analysis

- Read words with common spelling patterns
- Read high-frequency and sight words
- Read regularly spelled one-syllable words

Comprehension

- Recall details
- Respond to who, what, where, how questions

Writing

- Print legibly and space letters and words appropriately

Learn More -um and -unk Words

Guide a discussion that helps students recall yesterday's story. Say:

Our story was about brothers who cleaned their room.

- *What did they put in the trash?* (junk)
- *Which word family does* **junk** *belong to?* (-unk)

Then distribute pencils and the Day 2 activity. Say:

- *Point to the* **-um** *word family at the top of the page. Let's read the* **-um** *words together. Point to each word as we read:* **gum, sum, drum**.
- *Now point to the* **-unk** *word family. Let's read the* **-unk** *words together. Point to each word as we read:* **bunk, trunk, skunk**.
- *Look at number 1. It shows gum. What is the first sound in* **gum**? (/g/) *Which word part do you hear at the <u>end</u> of* **gum**? (/ŭm/) *Write the word* **gum** *in the boxes.*

Repeat the process for numbers 2 through 6. Then say:

- *Look at the words at the bottom of the page. Read each word. Circle the words that belong to the* **-um** *word family. Underline the words that belong to the* **-unk** *word family. Let's read the first word together:* **dunk**. *Which word family does* **dunk** *belong to?* (-unk) *Draw a line under* **dunk**.

Repeat the process for the remaining words.

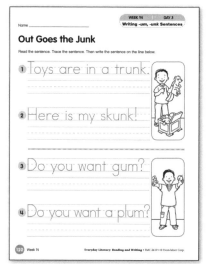

Day 2 activity

Day 3

SKILLS:

Phonics/ Word Analysis

- Read words with common spelling patterns
- Read high-frequency and sight words
- Read regularly spelled one-syllable words

Comprehension

- Recall details
- Respond to who, what, where, how questions

Writing

- Print legibly and space letters and words appropriately

Writing -um and -unk Sentences

Reread the Day 1 story. Then guide a discussion about the story by saying:

Our story was about tossing out junk.

- *What was broken?* (drum) *Which word family does* **drum** *belong to?* (-um)

Distribute pencils and the Day 3 activity. Say:

We are going to read, trace, and then write sentences that have **-um** *and* **-unk** *words.*

- *Point to the first sentence. Move your finger under each word as we read together:* **Toys are in a trunk**. *Which word is from the* **-unk** *word family?* (trunk) *Now trace the sentence, then write the sentence again on the line below. Put your pencil down when you are finished.*
- *Point to the next sentence. Let's read it together:* **Here is my skunk!** *Which word is from the* **-unk** *word family?* (skunk) *Trace the sentence, then write the sentence again on the line below. Put your pencil down when you are finished.*

After students complete sentence 2, have them read sentences 1 and 2 aloud. Repeat the process for sentences 3 and 4.

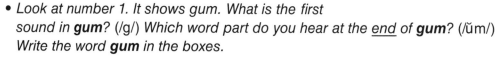

Day 3 activity

SKILLS:

Phonics/ Word Analysis
- Read words with common spelling patterns
- Read high-frequency and sight words

Comprehension
- Recall details
- Respond to who, what, where, how questions

Writing
- Print legibly and space letters and words appropriately

Reading *-um* and *-unk* Words

Reread the Day 1 story if necessary. Then guide a discussion about the story by saying:

The brothers in our story cleaned their room.

- *Where did they put their toys?* (in a trunk)
  What word family is the word **trunk** *from?* (-unk)

- *How would their mom feel about a mess?* (glum)
  What word family is **glum** *from?* (-um)

Distribute pencils and the Day 4 activity. Say:

Listen carefully and follow my directions.

- *Put your finger on the first sentence at the top of the page. Move your finger under each word as we read it together:* **I can hum.** *Underline the word from the* **-um** *word family.* (hum) *Draw a line to the picture that matches the sentence.*

Repeat the process for numbers 2 through 4. Then point to the word box at the bottom of the page and say:

- *Point to this word box. Let's read the words together:* **gum, chunk, plum.** *Each sentence below is missing one word. Look at the picture next to each sentence. Write one of the words from the word box to complete each sentence.*

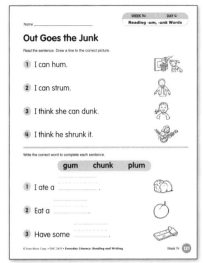

Day 4 activity

SKILLS:

Phonemic Awareness
- Recognize a new spoken word when a phoneme is added, changed, or removed

Phonics/ Word Analysis
- Read words with common spelling patterns

Oral Language Activity

Reinforce this week's word families by using a phoneme substitution activity. Introduce and model the call-and-response below.

All: *Let's make a word family; we'll have fun.*
All: *Let's make a word family;* **-unk** *is one.*

Students: *What's the word?*
Teacher: *The word is* **dunk.**
Students: *What do we change?*
Teacher: *Change /d/ to /j/.*
Students: **Junk!**
Teacher: **Junk** *is the word.*

Students: *What's the word?*
Teacher: *The word is* **junk.**
Students: *What do we change?*
Teacher: *Change /j/ to /s/.*
Students: **Sunk!**
Teacher: **Sunk** *is the word.*

Continue the chant using **bunk, gunk, trunk, skunk.**

Then repeat the chant using **-um** family words: /h/ hum, /m/ mum, /s/ sum, /pl/ plum, /b/ bum, /sw/ swum, etc.

Extension: Write **-um** and **-unk** words on index cards. Recite the chant above using letter names instead of sounds. For example, say: *Change j to s.* After students say the new word, hold up the corresponding word card (**sunk**) as you say the word.

Home–School Connection p. 122 Spanish version available (see p. 2)

Out Goes the Junk

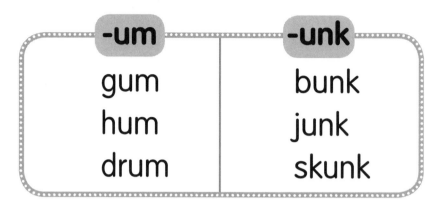

-um	-unk
gum	bunk
hum	junk
drum	skunk

Name _____

Out Goes the Junk

-um	-unk
gum	bunk
sum	trunk
drum	skunk

Write the correct word in the boxes.

1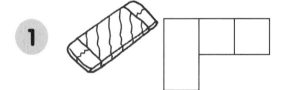

4

2

5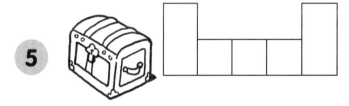

3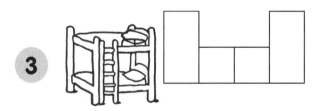

6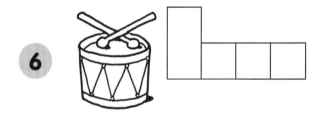

Circle the **-um** words. Underline the **-unk** words.

-um   -unk

dunk	hum	mum	junk	plum	hunk
flunk	chum	sunk	strum	plunk	glum

Out Goes the Junk

Read the sentence. Trace the sentence. Then write the sentence on the line below.

1 Toys are in a trunk.

2 Here is my skunk!

3 Do you want gum?

4 Do you want a plum?

Name _____

Out Goes the Junk

Read the sentence. Draw a line to the correct picture.

1 I can hum.

2 I can strum.

3 I think she can dunk.

4 I think he shrunk it.

Write the correct word to complete each sentence.

> **gum   chunk   plum**

1 I ate a _____.

2 Eat a _____.

3 Have some _____.

Name _____

Out Goes the Junk

What to Do
Read the story with your child and look at the picture together. Then have your child circle words in the story that end with **-um** and draw a line under words that end with **-unk**.

To Parents
This week your child learned to read and write words from the **-um** and **-unk** word families.

Mom was glum. Our room was a mess. So we made up our bunk beds. We put toys in the trunk. And we put junk into the trash—plunk!

What to Do Next
Work together with your child to write a story using words from the **-um** and **-unk** word families.

Review It

Word Family Words:
-ub: cub, club, rub, scrub, sub, tub
-ug: bug, hug, jug, mug, plug, rug, snug
-um: drum, glum, gum, hum, plum, sum
-unk: bunk, dunk, flunk, junk, skunk, sunk, trunk
High-Frequency Words: a, and, get, give, have, in, into, is, little, my, play, sit, stand, the, toy, wash, with, you

Day 1

SKILLS:
Phonemic Awareness
• Generate sounds from letter patterns
• Blend two to four phonemes into recognizable words

Phonics/Word Analysis
• Read words with common spelling patterns
• Read regularly spelled one-syllable words

Listening for Short *u* Word Families

Distribute the Day 1 activity and a pencil to each student. Then say:

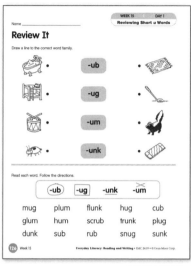

Day 1 activity

• *Let's review the short **u** word families we learned during the past few weeks. Point to each gray box as we read each word family ending together: **-ub, -ug, -um, -unk**. Now we'll match each picture to its word family. Point to the tub. Say **tub**.* (tub) *What word family does **tub** belong to?* (-ub) *What letters stand for /ŭb/?* (ub) *Draw a line from the tub to the correct word family.*

• *Point to the bunk beds. Say **bunk**.* (bunk) *What word family does **bunk** belong to?* (-unk) *What letters stand for /ŭnk/?* (unk) *Draw a line from the bunk beds to the correct word family.*

• *Point to the drum. Say **drum**.* (drum) *What word family does **drum** belong to?* (-um) *What letters stand for /ŭm/?* (um) *Draw a line from the drum to the correct word family.*

Repeat the process for the remaining picture words: **bug**, **rug**, **club**, **skunk**, and **gum**.

Discriminating *-ub, -ug, -um, unk*

Direct students' attention to the bottom half of the page. Then say:

• *These words belong to short **u** word families. We're going to read each word and follow the directions shown in the box. Let's start with the **-ub** word family. When you read a word that belongs to the **-ub** family, draw a circle around it. Do that now.* (pause) *Which words did you circle?* (sub, scrub, rub, cub)

• *Now look for words from the **-ug** word family. When you read a word that belongs to the **-ug** family, draw a box around it. Do that now.* (pause) *Which words did you box?* (mug, hug, snug, plug)

• *Now look for words from the **-unk** word family. When you read a word that belongs to the **-unk** family, draw a line under it. Do that now.* (pause) *Which words did you underline?* (dunk, flunk, trunk, sunk)

• *Now look for words from the **-um** word family. When you read a word that belongs to the **-um** family, write an **X** above it. Do that now.* (pause) *Which words did you mark with an **X**?* (glum, plum, hum)

Day 2

SKILLS:

Phonemic Awareness
- Segment onset and rime

Phonics/ Word Analysis
- Read words with common spelling patterns
- Read high-frequency and sight words
- Read regularly spelled one-syllable words

Writing
- Print legibly and space letters and words appropriately

Writing Short *u* Word Family Words

Distribute the Day 2 activity and a pencil to each student. Then say:

- *Look at the word endings in the box. Let's read them together: **-ub, -ug, -um, -unk**. Now look at the pictures below.*

- *Point to picture number 1. It shows a jug. Which word family does **jug** belong to? (-ug) Write the missing letters to finish the word **jug**.*

- *Point to picture number 2. It shows junk. Which word family does **junk** belong to? (-unk) Write the missing letters to finish the word **junk**.*

Repeat the process for the remaining words: **bug, bunk, plum, plug, sub, sum**. Then say:

- *Now we're going to read sentences and draw a line to the matching picture. Point to number 1. Let's read together: **I have a toy skunk. You have gum and a plum.** Draw a line to the picture that matches the sentences.*

Repeat the process for the remaining sentences.

Day 2 activity

Day 3

SKILLS:

Phonics/Word Analysis
- Read words with common spelling patterns
- Read regularly spelled one-syllable words

Writing
- Use developing knowledge of letter-sound correspondences to spell independently
- Print legibly and space letters and words appropriately

Reading Words with *-ub, -ug, -um, -unk*

Distribute the Day 3 activity and a pencil to each student. Say:

- *The words in the box belong to short **u** word families. Point to each word and read with me: **hum, rug, dunk, hug, sub, scrub, mug, tub, bunk, cub.***

- *Point to sentence number 1. Move your finger under each word as we read together: **I sit in the (blank)**. What does the picture show? (tub) Write **tub** to complete the sentence. Use the word box if you need help.*

- *Read sentence 2: **I play with a (blank)**. What does the picture show? (sub) Write **sub** in the sentence.*

- *Read sentence 3: **I wash and (blank)**. What does the picture show? (scrub) Write **scrub** in the sentence.*

- *Read sentence 4: **I stand on the (blank)**. What does the picture show? (rug) Write **rug** in the sentence.*

- *Read sentence 5: **I climb into my (blank)**. What does the picture show? (bunk) Write **bunk** in the sentence.*

- *Point to number 6. What do you see in the picture? (hug) Write a sentence about the picture. (Answers vary.) Then read your sentence to a partner.*

Day 3 activity

Everyday Literacy: Reading and Writing • EMC 2419 • © Evan-Moor Corp.

Day 4

SKILLS:

**Phonics/
Word Analysis**

- Read words with common spelling patterns
- Read high-frequency and sight words
- Read regularly spelled one-syllable words

Comprehension

- Describe a picture using complete sentences

Writing

- Use developing knowledge of letter-sound correspondences to spell independently
- Print legibly and space letters and words appropriately

Writing Short *u* Word Sentences

Distribute the Day 4 activity and pencils. Say:

- *Look at the first picture. What do you see? (a boy in the tub) Now look at the words in the first box. These words make up a sentence that tells about the picture. The words are out of order. Unscramble the words to write a sentence about the picture. Put your pencil down when you are finished.*

- *Look at the next picture. What do you see? (a skunk on a rug) Now look at the words in the box. These words make up a sentence that tells about the picture. The words are out of order. Unscramble the words to write a sentence about the picture. Put your pencil down when you are finished.*

- *Look at the words in the last box. Point to each word as we read it:* **bug**, **drum**. *Write a sentence that uses these words. Then draw a picture about your sentence.* (Answers vary.)

Day 4 activity

Day 5

SKILLS:

**Phonics/
Word Analysis**

- Read words with common spelling patterns
- Use context clues in decoding words

Phonics Game

Review the short **u** word families students learned this week by playing the following game.

Materials: 4 index cards per group, labeled **-ub**, **-ug**, **-um**, and **-unk**

How to Play: Pick a "mystery word" from the chart below and write its first letter (or blend) on the board. Have students in each group sort through their word family cards and find all the cards that can be added to that letter to form a word. For example, if you write **b** on the board, students should determine that they can form **bug**, **bum**, and **bunk**.

Then give students the mystery word's clue from the chart, and have each group decide what the mystery word is (e.g., "something small that flies and crawls" must be "bug") and the word family card that can be used to form it (**-ug**). Ask a volunteer from each group to hold up the correct card.

Mystery Word	Clue	Mystery Word	Clue
bug	something small that flies and crawls	hum	to sing with your mouth closed
jug	something that you can put water in	plum	a fruit
chum	a funny word for a friend	sunk	it would not float, so it _____
jig	a funny dance called a _____	wig	not real hair

Home–School Connection p. 130

Spanish version available (see p. 2)

Name _____

Review It

Draw a line to the correct word family.

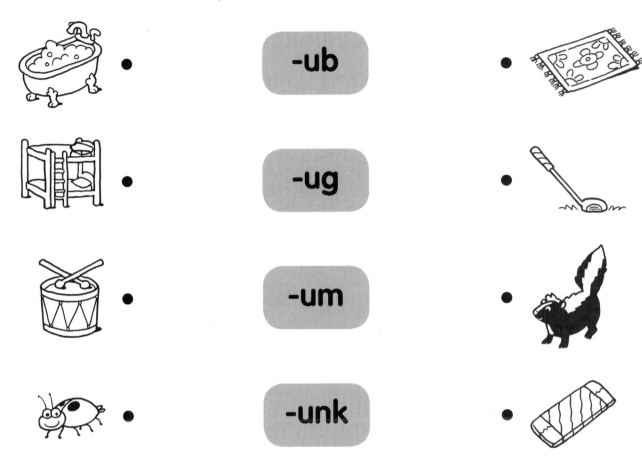

-ub

-ug

-um

-unk

Read each word. Follow the directions.

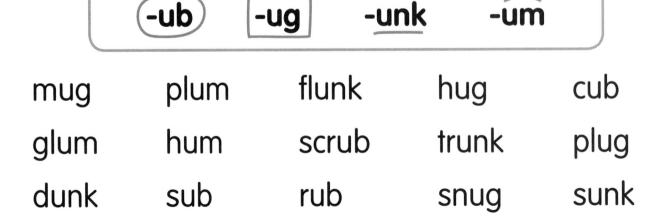

-ub   -ug   -unk   -um

mug	plum	flunk	hug	cub
glum	hum	scrub	trunk	plug
dunk	sub	rub	snug	sunk

Everyday Literacy: Reading and Writing • EMC 2419 • © Evan-Moor Corp.

Name _____

Write It

Which word family do you hear?
Write **ub**, **ug**, **um**, or **unk** to spell each word.

-ub   -ug   -um   -unk

  j _____

 pl _____

 j _____

 pl _____

 b _____

 s _____

 b _____

 s _____

Read the sentences. Draw a line to the correct picture.

1 I have a toy skunk.
You have gum and a plum.

2 I have a little cub.
I give my cub a hug.

Name _____

Read It

Read the words in the box. Write the correct word to complete each sentence.

hum	rug	dunk	hug	sub
scrub	mug	tub	bunk	cub

1 I sit in the _____.

2 I play with a _____.

3 I wash and _____.

4 I stand on the _____.

5 I climb into my _____.

Write a sentence about the picture.

6 _____

Name _____

Write It

Look at the picture.
Then use the words in the box to write a sentence on the lines.

> the I tub. in scrub

_____

_____

_____

> is on A skunk rug. the

_____

_____

_____

Use the words in the box to write a sentence. Then draw a picture.

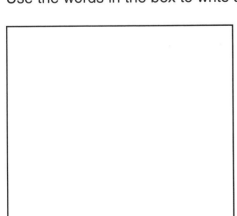

> bug   drum

_____

_____

_____

Name _____

Short u Word Families

Write **ub**, **ug**, **um**, or **unk** to finish each word.

WEEK 15

Home–School Connection

To Parents
This week your child reviewed how to read and write words from the **-ub**, **-ug**, **-um**, and **-unk** word families.

j _____

b _____

j _____

b _____

pl _____

pl _____

h _____

h _____

Read the sentence. Fill in the circle below the correct picture.

1 I have a plum.

○   ○

2 We see a bug.

○   ○

3 What is the sum?

○   ○

Everyday Literacy: Reading and Writing • EMC 2419 • © Evan-Moor Corp.

-ice
-ide

Slide, Glide, Ride on Ice

Word Families
-ice, -ide
Vocabulary
-ice: dice, ice, mice, nice, price, rice, slice, twice, vice
-ide: bride, glide, hide, ride, side, slide, tide, wide
High-Frequency Words: a, and, are, can, did, do, eat, here, I, is, it, on, ride, the, want, we, where, you

Day 1

SKILLS:

Phonemic Awareness
- Generate sounds from letter patterns
- Blend two to four phonemes into recognizable words

Phonics/ Word Analysis
- Read words with common spelling patterns
- Read high-frequency and sight words
- Read regularly spelled one-syllable words

Comprehension
- Identify story characters
- Identify main idea
- Respond to who, what, where, how questions

Introducing Long *i* Word Families: *-ice, -ide*

Distribute the Day 1 activity page. Say: *This week we are reading and writing two long **i** word families: /īce/ and /īde/.*

- *Point to the **-ice** box at the top of the page. Say /īs/. (/īs/) Point to the first word. It has two vowels, **i** and **e**. The **i** makes a long sound, /ī/. The **e** at the end does not make a sound; it is silent. Say the letter sounds with me: /m-ī-s/. Blend the sounds together: **mice**. Point to the next word: /r-ī-s/, **rice**. Point to the last word: /ī-s/, **ice**. What word part is the same in all of these words? (/īs/) These words belong to the **-ice** word family because they all end with **ice**.*

- *Now point to the **-ide** box. Say /īde/. (/īde/) Point to the first word. Say the letter sounds with me: /r-ī-d/, **ride**. Point to the next word: /h-ī-d/, **hide**. Point to the next word: /s-l-ī-d/, **slide**. What word part is the same? (/īd/) These words belong to the **-ide** word family because they all end with **ide**.*

Listening to the Story

Say: *Listen as I read you a story that has words from the **-ice** and the **-ide** word families. The title of this story is "Slide, Glide, Ride on Ice."*

It was a wintry night. A family of mice had a nice, warm place to hide. They ate their rice and went to sleep. Except for Mo. His eyes were wide open. Mo tiptoed outside to play on the ice. First, he would slide. Then, he would glide. He took a sled ride! When he went back inside, nobody knew he'd been gone. Mo had been as quiet as a mouse.

Thinking About the Story

Distribute pencils. Guide students in discussing the story. Say:

- *Who are the characters in this story? (a family of mice; Mo) What word part do you hear at the end of **mice**? (/īs/) Which word family does **mice** belong to? (-ice) Make a dot on the sleeping **mice**.*

- *What was this story about? (Mo wasn't sleepy, so he snuck outside to play). What did Mo do on the ice? (slide, glide, ride) What word part do you hear at the end of those words? (/īd/) Which word family do they belong to? (-ide) Write an **X** beside Mo **gliding**.*

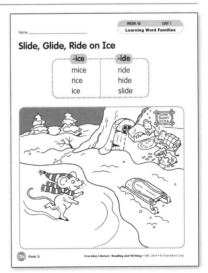

Day 1 picture

Day 2

SKILLS:

Phonemic Awareness

- Generate sounds from letter patterns
- Segment onset and rime

Phonics/ Word Analysis

- Read words with common spelling patterns
- Read high-frequency and sight words
- Read regularly spelled one-syllable words

Comprehension

- Recall details
- Respond to who, what, where, how questions

Writing

- Print legibly and space letters and words appropriately

Listening for *-ice* and *-ide* Words

Guide a discussion that helps students recall yesterday's story. Say:

Our story was about a family of mice.

- *What did the mice eat?* (rice) *Which word family do the words **mice** and **rice** belong to?* (-ice)

Then distribute pencils and the Day 2 activity. Say:

- *Point to the **-ice** word family at the top of the page. Let's read the **-ice** words together. Point to each word as we read: **mice**, **price**, **slice**.*

- *Now point to the **-ide** word family at the top of the page. Let's read the **-ide** words together. Point to each word as we read: **hide**, **ride**, **bride**.*

- *Look at number 1. It shows **hide**. What is the first sound in **hide**?* (/h/) *Which word part do you hear at the <u>end</u> of **hide**?* (/īde/) *Write the word **hide** in the boxes.*

Repeat the process for numbers 2 through 6. Then say:

- *Look at the words at the bottom of the page. Read each word. Circle the words that belong to the **-ice** word family. Underline the words that belong to the **-ide** word family. Let's read the first word together: **nice**. Which word family does **nice** belong to?* (-ice) *Circle the word **nice**.*

Repeat the process for the remaining words.

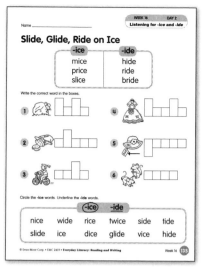

Day 2 activity

Day 3

SKILLS:

Phonics/ Word Analysis

- Read words with common spelling patterns
- Read high-frequency and sight words
- Read regularly spelled one-syllable words

Comprehension

- Recall details
- Respond to who, what, where, how questions

Writing

- Print legibly and space letters and words appropriately

Writing *-ice* and *-ide* Sentences

Reread the Day 1 story. Then guide a discussion about the story by saying:

Our story was about Mo the mouse. What did Mo do outside? (slide, glide, ride) *Which word family do the words **slide**, **glide**, and **ride** belong to?* (-ide)

Distribute pencils and the Day 3 activity. Say:

*We are going to read, trace, and then write sentences that have **-ice** and **-ide** words.*

- *Point to the first sentence. Move your finger under each word as we read together: **We are nice mice**. Which words are from the **-ice** word family?* (nice, mice) *Now trace the sentence, then write the sentence again on the line below. Put your pencil down when you are finished.*

- *Point to the next sentence. Let's read it together: **We eat rice**. Which word is from the **-ice** word family?* (rice) *Trace the sentence, then write the sentence again on the line below. Put your pencil down when you are finished.*

After students complete sentence 2, have them read sentences 1 and 2 aloud. Repeat the process for sentences 3 and 4.

Day 3 activity

SKILLS:
Phonics/
Word Analysis
- Read words with common spelling patterns
- Read high-frequency and sight words
- Read regularly spelled one-syllable words

Comprehension
- Recall details
- Respond to who, what, where, how questions

Writing
- Print legibly and space letters and words appropriately

Reading *-ice* and *-ide* Words

Reread the Day 1 story if necessary. Then guide a discussion about the story by saying:

There was a mouse named Mo in our story.

- *What did he eat?* (rice) *What word family is that word from?* (-ice)

- *What did Mo like to do on the ice?* (slide, glide, ride a sled) *What word family are those words from?* (-ide)

Distribute pencils and the Day 4 activity. Say:

Listen carefully and follow my directions.

- *Put your finger on the first question at the top of the page. Move your finger under each word as we read it together:* **Where did it hide?** *Underline the word from the* **-ide** *word family.* (hide) *Draw a line to the picture that matches the question.*

Repeat the process for numbers 2 through 4. Then point to the word box at the bottom of the page and say:

- *Point to this word box. Let's read the words together:* **bride, price, rice.** *Each sentence below is missing one word. Look at the picture next to each sentence. Write one of the words from the word box to complete each sentence.*

Day 4 activity

SKILLS:
Phonemic
Awareness
- Recognize a new spoken word when a phoneme is added, changed, or removed

Phonics/
Word Analysis
- Read words with common spelling patterns

Oral Language Activity

Reinforce this week's word families by using a phoneme substitution activity. Introduce and model the call-and-response below.

All: *Let's make a word family; we'll have fun.*
All: *Let's make a word family;* **-ice** *is one.*

Students: *What's the word?*
Teacher: *The word is* **mice.**
Students: *What do we change?*
Teacher: *Change* /m/ *to* /r/.
Students: **Rice!**
Teacher: **Rice** *is the word.*

Students: *What's the word?*
Teacher: *The word is* **rice.**
Students: *What do we change?*
Teacher: *Change* /r/ *to* /pr/.
Students: **Price!**
Teacher: **Price** *is the word.*

Continue the chant using: **nice, twice, slice, vice.**

Then repeat the chant using **-ide** family words: /r/ *ride,* /h/ *hide,* /s/ *side,* /w/ *wide,* /sl/ *slide,* /gl/ *glide,* etc.

Extension: Write **-ice** and **-ide** words on index cards. Recite the chant above using letter names instead of sounds. For example, say: *Change* **r** *to* **pr**. After students say the new word, hold up the corresponding word card (**price**) as you say the word.

Home–School Connection p. 138
Spanish version available (see p. 2)

Slide, Glide, Ride on Ice

-ice	-ide
mice	ride
rice	hide
ice	slide

Everyday Literacy: Reading and Writing • EMC 2419 • © Evan-Moor Corp.

Name _____

Slide, Glide, Ride on Ice

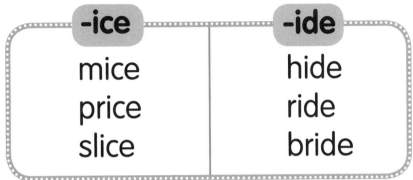

-ice	**-ide**
mice	hide
price	ride
slice	bride

Write the correct word in the boxes.

 1

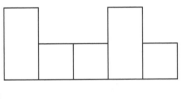 4

 2

 5

 3

 6

Circle the **-ice** words. Underline the **-ide** words.

(ice) -ide

nice	wide	rice	twice	side	tide
slide	ice	dice	glide	vice	hide

Slide, Glide, Ride on Ice

Read the sentence. Trace the sentence. Then write the sentence on the line below.

1 We are nice mice.

2 We eat rice.

3 I ride and ride.

4 I slide and glide.

Everyday Literacy: Reading and Writing • EMC 2419 • © Evan-Moor Corp.

Name _____

Slide, Glide, Ride on Ice

Read the question. Draw a line to the correct picture.

1 Where did it hide?

2 Can you slide on it?

3 Do you want a slice?

4 Do you want the dice?

Write the correct word to complete each sentence.

bride   price   rice

1 Here is the _____ .

2 Here is the _____ .

3 Here is the _____ .

Name _____

Slide, Glide, Ride on Ice

What to Do

Read the story with your child and look at the picture together. Then have your child circle words in the story that end with **-ice** and draw a line under words that end with **-ide**.

To Parents
This week your child learned to read and write words from the **-ice** and **-ide** word families.

The mice ate their rice. They went to sleep.
Not Mo. He went out on the ice to slide and glide!
Mo went back inside. He was as quiet as a mouse.

What to Do Next

Work together with your child to write a story using words from the **-ice** and **-ide** word families.

WEEK 17

-old
-ow

Snow Day

Word Families
-old, -ow

Vocabulary
-old: bold, cold, fold, gold, hold, old, scold, sold, told
-ow: bow, blow, crow, grow, know, low, mow, row, show, slow, snow, tow

High-Frequency Words: a, are, at, call, for, has, hers, him, his, I, in, is, it, look, mine, the, this, to, will, yours

---

Day 1

SKILLS:

Phonemic Awareness
- Generate sounds from letter patterns
- Blend two to four phonemes into recognizable words

Phonics/ Word Analysis
- Read words with common spelling patterns
- Read high-frequency and sight words
- Read regularly spelled one-syllable words

Comprehension
- Identify story characters
- Identify main idea
- Respond to who, what, where, how questions

Introducing Long *o* Word Families: *-old, -ow*

Distribute the Day 1 activity page. Say: *This week we are reading and writing two long* **o** *word families: /ōld/ and /ōw/l/.*

- *Point to the* **-old** *box at the top of the page. Say /ōld/. (/ōld/) Point to the first word. Say the letter sounds with me: /k-ō-l-d/. Blend the sounds together:* **cold***. Point to the next word: /h-ō-l-d/,* **hold***. Point to the last word: /s-k-ō-l-d/,* **scold***. What word part is the same in all of these words? (/ōld/) These words belong to the* **-old** *word family.*

- *Now point to the* **-ow** *box. Say /ō/. (/ō/) Point to the first word. Say the letter sounds with me: /t-ō/,* **tow***. Point to the next word: /s-n-ō/,* **snow***. Point to the last word. The* **k** *is silent: /n-ō/,* **know***. What word part is the same in all of these words? (/ō/) These words belong to the* **-ow** *word family.*

Listening to the Story

Listen as I read you a story that has words from the **-old** *and the* **-ow** *word families. The title of this story is "Snow Day."*

Last night, I heard the cold wind blow. This morning, there's snow! Maybe my school will declare it a snow day and I can stay home. Dad says it's time for me to get ready for school. "Is it a snow day?" I ask. Dad says it's not. I quickly get dressed and eat so Dad does not scold me for being late. I go outside into the cold and see Dad under the hood of the car. "It won't start," he said. "I had to call for a tow. It could take hours. Looks like it's a snow day for you after all," he smiled.

Thinking About the Story

Distribute pencils. Guide students in discussing the story. Say:

- *What kind of day is it?* (cold, snowy) *What word part do you hear at the end of* **cold***? (/ōld/) Which word family does* **cold** *belong to?* (-old) *Make a dot on something that is* **cold***.*

- *What was this story about?* (a car that won't start on a snowy morning) *How will they get the car started?* (call a tow truck) *What word part do you hear at the end of* **snow** *and* **tow***? (/ō/) Which word family do those words belong to?* (-ow) *Write an* **X** *on something that needed a* **tow***.*

Day 1 picture

Day 2

SKILLS:

Phonemic Awareness
- Generate sounds from letter patterns
- Segment onset and rime

Phonics/ Word Analysis
- Read words with common spelling patterns
- Read high-frequency and sight words
- Read regularly spelled one-syllable words

Comprehension
- Recall details
- Respond to who, what, where, how questions

Writing
- Print legibly and space letters and words appropriately

Learn More *-old* and *-ow* Words

Guide a discussion that helps students recall yesterday's story. Say:

Our story was about a snowy morning.

- *Why did the girl get dressed and eat quickly?* (so her dad would not scold her for being late)
- *Which word family does* **scold** *belong to?* (-old)

Then distribute pencils and the Day 2 activity. Say:

- *Point to the* **-old** *word family at the top of the page. Let's read the* **-old** *words together. Point to each word as we read:* **gold, fold, sold.**
- *Now point to the* **-ow** *word family at the top of the page. Let's read the* **-ow** *words together. Point to each word as we read:* **bow, mow, crow.**
- *Look at number 1. It shows a bow. What is the first sound in* **bow**? (/b/) *Which word part do you hear at the* <u>end</u> *of* **bow**? (/ō/) *Write the word* **bow** *in the boxes.*

Repeat the process for numbers 2 through 6. Then say:

- *Look at the words at the bottom of the page. Read each word. Circle the words that belong to the* **-old** *word family. Underline the words that belong to the* **-ow** *word family. Let's read the first word together:* **told.** *Which word family does* **told** *belong to?* (-old) *Circle the word* **told.**

Repeat the process for the remaining words.

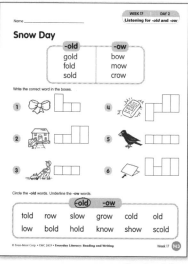

Day 2 activity

Day 3

SKILLS:

Phonics/ Word Analysis
- Read words with common spelling patterns
- Read high-frequency and sight words

Comprehension
- Recall details
- Respond to who, what, where, how questions
- Read regularly spelled one-syllable words

Writing
- Print legibly and space letters and words appropriately

Writing *-old* and *-ow* Sentences

Reread the Day 1 story. Then guide a discussion about the story by saying:

Our story was about a girl who heard a cold wind blow. What did the cold wind bring? (snow) *Which word family does* **snow** *belong to?* (-ow)

Distribute pencils and the Day 3 activity. Say:

We are going to read, trace, and then write sentences that have **-old** *and* **-ow** *words.*

- *Point to the first sentence. Move your finger under each word as we read together:* **This is cold.** *Which word is from the* **-old** *word family?* (cold) *Now trace the sentence, then write the sentence again on the line below. Put your pencil down when you are finished.*
- *Point to the next sentence. Let's read it together:* **It is cold to hold.** *Which words are from the* **-old** *word family?* (cold, hold) *Trace the sentence, then write the sentence again on the line below. Put your pencil down when you are finished.*

After students complete sentence 2, have them read sentences 1 and 2 aloud. Repeat the process for sentences 3 and 4.

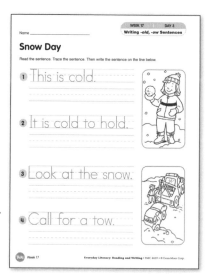

Day 3 activity

Everyday Literacy: Reading and Writing • EMC 2419 • © Evan-Moor Corp.

Day 4

SKILLS:
**Phonics/
Word Analysis**
- Read words with common spelling patterns
- Read high-frequency and sight words
- Read regularly spelled one-syllable words

Comprehension
- Recall details
- Respond to who, what, where, how questions

Writing
- Print legibly and space letters and words appropriately

Reading *-old* and *-ow* Words

Reread the Day 1 story if necessary. Then guide a discussion about the story by saying:

The dad in our story had car trouble.

- *What did he do when the car wouldn't start?* (looked under the hood; called a tow truck) *What word family is **tow** from?* (-ow)

Distribute pencils and the Day 4 activity. Say:

Listen carefully and follow my directions.

- *Put your finger on the first sentence at the top of the page. Move your finger under each word as we read it together: **Yours are old**. Underline the word from the **-old** word family. (old) Draw a line to the picture that matches the sentence.*

Repeat the process for numbers 2 through 4. Then point to the word box at the bottom of the page and say:

- *Point to this word box. Let's read the words together: **scold**, **hold**, **show**. Each sentence below is missing one word. Look at the picture next to each sentence. Write one of the words from the word box to complete each sentence.*

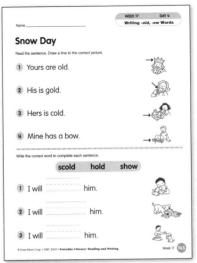

Day 4 activity

Day 5

SKILLS:
**Phonemic
Awareness**
- Recognize a new spoken word when a phoneme is added, changed, or removed

**Phonics/
Word Analysis**
- Read words with common spelling patterns

Oral Language Activity

Reinforce this week's word families by using a phoneme substitution activity. Introduce and model the call-and-response below.

All: *Let's make a word family; we'll have fun.*
All: *Let's make a word family; **-old** is one.*

Students: *What's the word?*
Teacher: *The word is **told**.*
Students: *What do we change?*
Teacher: *Change /t/ to /k/.*
Students: ***Cold!***
Teacher: ***Cold** is the word.*

Students: *What's the word?*
Teacher: *The word is **cold**.*
Students: *What do we change?*
Teacher: *Change /k/ to /h/.*
Students: ***Hold!***
Teacher: ***Hold** is the word.*

Continue the chant using **bold**, **fold**, **mold**, **sold**.

Then repeat the chant using **-ow** family words: r/ *row*, /b/ *bow*, /l/ *low*, /sn/ *snow*, /gr/ *grow*, /gl/ *glow*, /n/ *know*, etc.

Extension: Write **-old** and **-ow** words on index cards. Recite the chant above using letter names instead of sounds. For example, say: *Change **c** to **h***. After students say the new word, hold up the corresponding word card (**hold**) as you say the word.

**Home–School
Connection p. 146**
Spanish version available (see p. 2)

Name _____

Snow Day

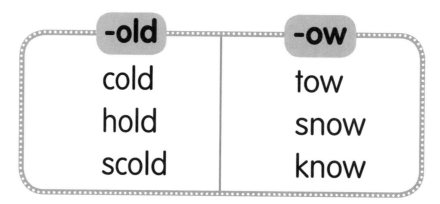

-old	**-ow**
cold	tow
hold	snow
scold	know

Everyday Literacy: Reading and Writing • EMC 2419 • © Evan-Moor Corp.

Name _____

Snow Day

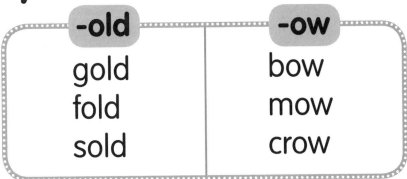

-old	**-ow**
gold	bow
fold	mow
sold	crow

Write the correct word in the boxes.

1

2

3

4

5

6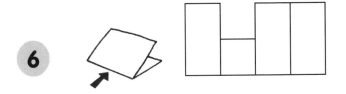

Circle the **-old** words. Underline the **-ow** words.

(-old)	-ow

told	row	slow	grow	cold	old
low	bold	hold	know	show	scold

Name _____

Snow Day

Read the sentence. Trace the sentence. Then write the sentence on the line below.

1 This is cold.

2 It is cold to hold.

3 Look at the snow.

4 Call for a tow.

Snow Day

Read the sentence. Draw a line to the correct picture.

1 Yours are old.

2 His is gold.

3 Hers is cold.

4 Mine has a bow.

Write the correct word to complete each sentence.

scold   hold   show

1 I will _____ him.

2 I will _____ him.

3 I will _____ him.

Snow Day

What to Do
Read the story with your child and look at the picture together. Then have your child circle words in the story that end with **-old** and draw a line under words that end with **-ow**.

To Parents
This week your child learned to read and write words from the **-old** and **-ow** word families.

A cold wind did blow. Now we have snow.
Dad will scold me if I hold the door open. Oh no!
The car won't start. Call for a tow. No school today!

What to Do Next
Work together with your child to write a story using words from the **-old** and **-ow** word families.

-ue -une

Dune Lake

Word Families
-ue; -une

Vocabulary
-ue: blue, clue, cue, due, flue, glue, Sue, true
-une: dune, June, prune, tune

High-Frequency Words: a, am, book, go, happy, have, I, is, in, like, the, reads, some, we, will

Day 1

SKILLS:

Phonemic Awareness
• Generate sounds from letter patterns
• Blend two to four phonemes into recognizable words

Phonics/ Word Analysis
• Read words with common spelling patterns
• Read high-frequency and sight words
• Read regularly spelled one-syllable words

Comprehension
• Identify story characters
• Identify main idea
• Respond to who, what, where, how questions

Introducing Long *u* Word Families: *-ue, -une*

Distribute the Day 1 activity page. Say: *This week we are reading and writing two long **u** word families: /ūe/ and /ūne/.*

• *Point to the **-ue** box at the top of the page. Say /o͞o/. (/o͞o/) Point to the first word. It has two vowels, **u** and **e**. The **u** makes a long sound: /o͞o/. The **e** at the end does not make a sound; it is silent. Say the letter sounds with me: /b-l-o͞o/. Blend the sounds together: **blue**. Point to the next word: /d-o͞o/, **due**. Point to the last word: /t-r-o͞o/, **true**. What word part is the same in all of these words? (/o͞o/) These words belong to the **-ue** word family.*

• *Now point to the **-une** box. Say /o͞on/. (/o͞on/) Point to the first word. Say the letter sounds with me: /j-o͞o-n/, **June**. Point to the next word: /t-o͞o-n/, **tune**. Point to the last word: /d-o͞o-n/, **dune**. What word part is the same in all of these words? (/o͞on/) These words belong to the **-une** word family.*

Listening to the Story

Say: *Listen as I read you a story that has words from the **-ue** and the **-une** word families. The title of this story is "Dune Lake."*

It's the month of June, and Sue and her family are going to stay in a cabin at Dune Lake. Sue checks out library books to bring along. They won't be due for three weeks, so she can keep them the whole time she's at the cabin. Sue likes to read nonfiction, or things that are true. She hums a happy tune as she thinks about lying under the sun and reading a book beside the blue water in Dune Lake.

Thinking About the Story

Distribute pencils. Guide students in discussing the story. Say:

• *Who is the main character in this story? (Sue) What word part do you hear at the end of **Sue**? (/o͞o/) Which word family does the word **Sue** belong to: **-ue** or **-une**? (-ue) Make a dot on **Sue**.*

• *What was this story about? (Sue gets some books to take to Dune Lake.) When does her family go to Dune Lake? (June) What word part do you hear at the end of **dune** and **June**? (/o͞on/) Which word family do those words belong to? (-une) Write an **X** on the **dune**.*

Day 1 picture

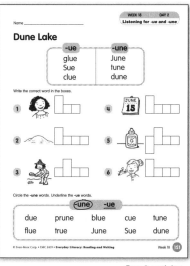

Day 2

SKILLS:

Phonemic Awareness
- Generate sounds from letter patterns
- Segment onset and rime

Phonics/ Word Analysis
- Read words with common spelling patterns
- Read high-frequency and sight words
- Read regularly spelled one-syllable words

Comprehension
- Recall details
- Respond to who, what, where, how questions

Writing
- Print legibly and space letters and words appropriately

Listening for *-ue* and *-une* Words

Guide a discussion that helps students recall yesterday's story. Say:

Our story was about Sue's trip to Dune Lake.

- *What kind of books did she take there?* (nonfiction; books that are true) *Which word family do the words **true** and **Sue** belong to?* (-ue)

Then distribute pencils and the Day 2 activity. Say:

- *Point to the **-ue** word family at the top of the page. Let's read the **-ue** words together. Point to each word as we read: **glue, Sue, clue.***

- *Now point to the **-une** word family at the top of the page. Let's read the **-une** words together. Point to each word as we read: **June, tune, dune.***

- *Look at number 1. It shows **Sue**. What is the first sound in **Sue**?* (/s/) *Which word part do you hear at the <u>end</u> of **Sue**?* (/o͞o/) *Write the word **Sue** in the boxes.*

Repeat the process for numbers 2 through 6. Then say:

- *Look at the words at the bottom of the page. Read each word. Circle the words that belong to the **-une** word family. Underline the words that belong to the **-ue** word family. Let's read the first word together: **due**. Which word family does **due** belong to?* (-ue) *Draw a line under **due**.*

Repeat the process for the remaining words.

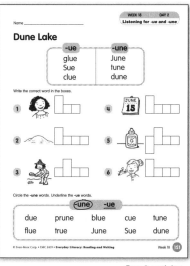

Day 2 activity

Day 3

SKILLS:

Phonics/ Word Analysis
- Read words with common spelling patterns
- Read high-frequency and sight words
- Read regularly spelled one-syllable words

Comprehension
- Recall details
- Respond to who, what, where, how questions

Writing
- Print legibly and space letters and words appropriately

Writing *-ue* and *-une* Sentences

Reread the Day 1 story. Then guide a discussion about the story by saying:

Our story was about a family's trip to Dune Lake.

- *In what month did Sue's family go to Dune Lake?* (June) *Which word family do the words **June** and **dune** belong to?* (-une)

Distribute pencils and the Day 3 activity. Say:

*We are going to read, trace, and then write sentences that have **-ue** and **-une** words.*

- *Point to the first sentence. Move your finger under each word as we read together: **I am happy in June**. Which word is from the **-une** word family?* (June) *Now trace the sentence, then write the sentence again on the line below. Put your pencil down when you are finished.*

- *Point to the next sentence. Let's read it together: **I hum a tune**. Which word is from the **-une** word family?* (tune) *Trace the sentence, then write the sentence again on the line below. Put your pencil down when you are finished.*

After students complete sentence 2, have them read sentences 1 and 2 aloud. Repeat the process for sentences 3 and 4.

Day 3 activity

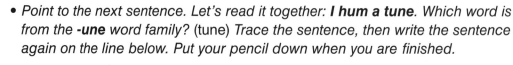

Day 4

SKILLS:
Phonics/ Word Analysis
- Read words with common spelling patterns
- Read high-frequency and sight words
- Read regularly spelled one-syllable words

Comprehension
- Recall details
- Respond to who, what, where, how questions

Writing
- Print legibly and space letters and words appropriately

Reading *-ue* and *-une* Words

Reread the Day 1 story if necessary. Then guide a discussion about the story by saying:

There was a girl in our story.

- *What was the girl's name?* (Sue)
- *What word family is that name from?* (-ue)
- *When did the story take place?* (June)
- *What word family is* **June** *from?* (-une)

Distribute pencils and the Day 4 activity. Say:

Listen carefully and follow my directions.

- *Put your finger on the first sentence at the top of the page. Move your finger under each word as we read it together:* **I have some glue**. *Underline the word from the* **-ue** *word family.* (glue) *Draw a line to the picture that matches the sentence.*

Repeat the process for numbers 2 through 4. Then point to the word box at the bottom of the page and say:

- *Point to this word box. Let's read the words together:* **blue, dune, June**. *Each sentence below is missing one word. Look at the picture next to each sentence. Write one of the words from the word box to complete each sentence.*

Day 4 activity

Day 5

SKILLS:
Phonemic Awareness
- Recognize a new spoken word when a phoneme is added, changed, or removed

Phonics/ Word Analysis
- Read words with common spelling patterns

Oral Language Activity

Reinforce this week's word families by using a phoneme substitution activity. Introduce and model the call-and-response below.

All: *Let's make a word family; we'll have fun.*
All: *Let's make a word family;* **-une** *is one.*

Students: *What's the word?*
Teacher: *The word is* **June**.
Students: *What do we change?*
Teacher: *Change /j/ to /d/.*
Students: **Dune!**
Teacher: **Dune** *is the word.*

Students: *What's the word?*
Teacher: *The word is* **dune**.
Students: *What do we change?*
Teacher: *Change /d/ to /pr/.*
Students: **Prune!**
Teacher: **Prune** *is the word.*

Continue the chant using **tune**.

Then repeat the chant using **-ue** family words: /s/ Sue, /bl/ blue, /k/ cue, /d/ due, /fl/ flue, /tr/ true, /gl/ glue, /h/ hue.

Extension: Write **-une** and **-ue** words on index cards. Recite the chant above using letter names instead of sounds. For example, say: *Change* **d** *to* **pr**. After students say the new word, hold up the corresponding word card (**prune**) as you say the word.

Name _____

Dune Lake

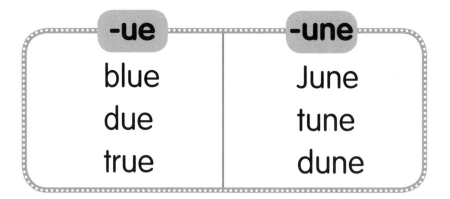

-ue	-une
blue	June
due	tune
true	dune

Name _____

Dune Lake

-ue	**-une**
glue	June
Sue	tune
clue	dune

Write the correct word in the boxes.

1

2

3

4

5

6

Circle the **-une** words. Underline the **-ue** words.

(-une) -ue

due	prune	blue	cue	tune
flue	true	June	Sue	dune

Writing -ue, -une Sentences

Name _____

Dune Lake

Read the sentence. Trace the sentence. Then write the sentence on the line below.

1 I am happy in June.

2 I hum a tune.

3 Sue reads a book.

4 The book is true.

Everyday Literacy: Reading and Writing • EMC 2419 • © Evan-Moor Corp.

Dune Lake

Read the sentence. Draw a line to the correct picture.

1 I have some glue.

2 I have a prune.

3 The sky is blue.

4 The book is true.

Write the correct word to complete each sentence.

blue   dune   June

1 We will climb the _____ .

2 We like the _____ lake.

3 We will go in _____ .

Name _____

Dune Lake

What to Do

Read the story with your child and look at the picture together. Then have your child circle words in the story that end with **-une** and draw a line under words that end with **-ue**.

To Parents
This week your child learned to read and write words from the **-une** and **-ue** word families.

It's June! Sue is going to Dune Lake.
She likes true books. So she will bring some to read.
Sue thinks about the blue lake. She hums a tune.

What to Do Next

Work together with your child to write a story using words from the **-une** and **-ue** word families.

Everyday Literacy: Reading and Writing • EMC 2419 • © Evan-Moor Corp.

At the Beach

Word Families
-each, -ear

Vocabulary
-each: beach, bleach, peach, preach, reach, teach
-ear: clear, dear, fear, gear, hear, near, spear, tear, year

High-Frequency Words: can, can't, baby, he, hear, here, how, I, is, it, know, me, old, one, she, the, to, which, will

Introducing Long *e* Word Families: *-each, -ear*

Distribute the Day 1 activity page. Say: *This week we are reading and writing two long **e** word families: /ēch/ and /ēr/.*

• *Point to the **-each** box at the top of the page. Say /ēch/. (/ēch/) Point to the first word. It has the vowels **e** and **a** next to each other. The **e** is first and makes a long sound: /ē/. The **a** is silent. Say the letter sounds with me: /b-ē-ch/. Blend the sounds together: **beach**. Point to the next word: /t-ē-ch/, **teach**. Point to the last word: /r-ē-ch/, **reach**. What word part is the same? (/ēch/) These words belong to the **-each** word family.*

• *Now point to the **-ear** box. Say /ēr/. (/ēr/) Point to the first word. Say the letter sounds with me: /y-ē-r/, **year**. Point to the next word: /f-ē-r/, **fear**. Point to the next word: /h-ē-r/, **hear**. What word part is the same in all of these words? (/ēr/) These words belong to the **-ear** word family.*

Listening to the Story

Say: *Listen as I read you a story that has words from the **-each** and the **-ear** word families. The title of this story is "At the Beach."*

> *I go to my dad's every year during summer break. He lives near the beach and teaches me water sports. This year, he is teaching me how to surf. At first, I had a fear of the big waves, but that went away fast. Now I jump onto the surfboard and ride the waves clear to the shore. I can't wait until next year—Dad's going to teach me how to water-ski!*

Thinking About the Story

Distribute pencils. Guide students in discussing the story. Say:

• *Where does this story take place? (the beach) What word part do you hear at the end of **beach** and **teach**? (/ēch/) Which word family do those words belong to: **-each** or **-ear**? (-each) Make a dot on someone who likes the **beach**.*

• *When will the boy learn to water-ski? (next year) What word part do you hear at the end of **year**? (/ēr/) Which word family does it belong to? (-ear) Write an **X** beside something the boy used to **fear**.*

Day 1 picture

SKILLS:

Phonemic Awareness
- Generate sounds from letter patterns
- Segment onset and rime

Phonics/ Word Analysis
- Read words with common spelling patterns
- Read high-frequency and sight words
- Read regularly spelled one-syllable words

Comprehension
- Recall details
- Respond to who, what, where, how questions

Writing
- Print legibly and space letters and words appropriately

Listening for *-each* and *-ear* Words

Guide a discussion that helps students recall yesterday's story. Say:

Our story was about a boy who visited his dad.

- *Where did his dad live? (near the beach) Which word family does* **beach** *belong to? (-each)*

Then distribute pencils and the Day 2 activity. Say:

- *Point to the* **-each** *word family at the top of the page. Let's read the* **-each** *words together. Point to each word as we read:* **teach, beach, peach.**

- *Now point to the* **-ear** *word family at the top of the page. Let's read the* **-ear** *words together. Point to each word as we read:* **tear, year, spear.**

- *Look at number 1. It shows a beach. What is the first sound in* **beach**? *(/b/) Which word part do you hear at the <u>end</u> of* **beach**? *(/ēch/) Write the word* **beach** *in the boxes.*

Repeat the process for numbers 2 through 6. Then say:

- *Look at the words at the bottom of the page. Read each word. Circle the words that belong to the* **-each** *word family. Underline the words that belong to the* **-ear** *word family. Let's read the first word together:* **dear**. *Which word family does* **dear** *belong to? (-ear) Draw a line under* **dear**.

Repeat the process for the remaining words.

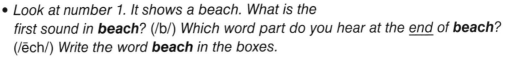

Day 2 activity

SKILLS:

Phonics/ Word Analysis
- Read words with common spelling patterns
- Read high-frequency and sight words
- Read regularly spelled one-syllable words

Comprehension
- Recall details
- Respond to who, what, where, how questions

Writing
- Print legibly and space letters and words appropriately

Writing *-each* and *-ear* Sentences

Reread the Day 1 story. Then guide a discussion about the story by saying:

Our story was about a boy who learned to surf.

- *When will his dad teach him to water-ski? (next year) Which word family does* **year** *belong to? (-ear)*

Distribute pencils and the Day 3 activity. Say:

We are going to read, trace, and then write sentences that have **-each** *and* **-ear** *words.*

- *Point to the first sentence. Move your finger under each word as we read together:* **The beach is near**. *Which word is from the* **-ear** *word family? (near) Which word is from the* **-each** *word family? (beach) Now trace the sentence, then write the sentence again on the line below. Put your pencil down when you are finished.*

- *Point to the next sentence. Let's read it together:* **I can hear it**. *Which word is from the* **-ear** *word family? (hear) Trace the sentence, then write the sentence again on the line below. Put your pencil down when you are finished.*

After students complete sentence 2, have them read sentences 1 and 2 aloud. Repeat the process for sentences 3 and 4.

Day 3 activity

Everyday Literacy: Reading and Writing • EMC 2419 • © Evan-Moor Corp.

Day 4

SKILLS:

**Phonics/
Word Analysis**

- Read words with common spelling patterns
- Read high-frequency and sight words
- Read regularly spelled one-syllable words

Comprehension

- Recall details
- Respond to who, what, where, how questions

Writing

- Print legibly and space letters and words appropriately

Reading -*each* and -*ear* Words

Reread the Day 1 story if necessary. Then guide a discussion about the story by saying:

There were a boy and his dad in our story.

- *Where did they go together? (beach) What word family is that word from? (-each)*
- *What did the boy feel about big waves at first? (He felt fear.) What word family is **fear** from? (-ear)*

Distribute pencils and the Day 4 activity. Say:
Listen carefully and follow my directions.

- *Put your finger on the first sentence at the top of the page. Move your finger under each word as we read it together: **Which one is near?** Underline the word from the **-ear** word family. (near) Draw a line to the picture that matches the sentence.*

Repeat the process for numbers 2 through 4. Then point to the word box at the bottom of the page and say:

- *Point to this word box. Let's read the words together: **reach**, **hear**, **year**. Each sentence below is missing one word. Look at the picture next to each sentence. Write one of the words from the word box to complete each sentence.*

Day 4 activity

Day 5

SKILLS:

**Phonemic
Awareness**

- Recognize a new spoken word when a phoneme is added, changed, or removed

**Phonics/
Word Analysis**

- Read words with common spelling patterns

Oral Language Activity

Reinforce this week's word families by using a phoneme substitution activity. Introduce and model the call-and-response below.

All: *Let's make a word family; we'll have fun.*
All: *Let's make a word family; **-each** is one.*

Students: *What's the word?*
Teacher: *The word is **teach**.*
Students: *What do we change?*
Teacher: *Change /t/ to /r/.*
Students: ***Reach!***
Teacher: ***Reach** is the word.*

Students: *What's the word?*
Teacher: *The word is **reach**.*
Students: *What do we change?*
Teacher: *Change /r/ to /b/.*
Students: ***Beach!***
Teacher: ***Beach** is the word.*

Continue the chant using **peach**, **bleach**, **preach**, **breach**.

Then repeat the chant using **-ear** family words: /y/ year, /d/ dear, /h/ hear, /n/ near, /t/ tear, /f/ fear, /g/ gear, etc.

Extension: Write **-each** and **-ear** words on index cards. Recite the chant above using letter names instead of sounds. For example, say: *Change **r** to **b**.* After students say the new word, hold up the corresponding word card (**beach**) as you say the word.

**Home–School
Connection p. 162**
Spanish version
available (see p. 2)

Name _____

At the Beach

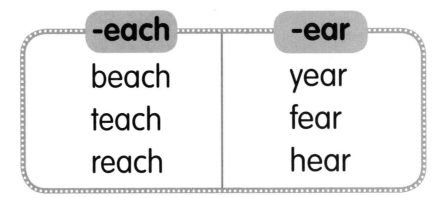

-each	-ear
beach	year
teach	fear
reach	hear

Everyday Literacy: Reading and Writing • EMC 2419 • © Evan-Moor Corp.

Name _____

At the Beach

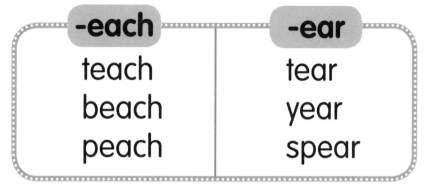

-each	-ear
teach	tear
beach	year
peach	spear

Write the correct word in the boxes.

1

2

3

4

5

6

Circle the **-each** words. Underline the **-ear** words.

(-each) -ear

dear   teach   clear   reach   beach   near

gear   bleach   fear   hear   peach   preach

Name _____

At the Beach

Read the sentence. Trace the sentence. Then write the sentence on the line below.

1 The beach is near.

2 I can hear it.

3 Here is the beach.

4 Dad will teach me.

Everyday Literacy: Reading and Writing • EMC 2419 • © Evan-Moor Corp.

Name _____

At the Beach

Read the sentence. Draw a line to the correct picture.

1 Which one is near?

2 Which one is clear?

3 I know how to reach it.

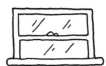

4 I know how to teach it.

Write the correct word to complete each sentence.

reach   hear   year

1 I _____ the baby.

2 He can't _____ it.

3 She is one _____ old.

Name _____

At the Beach

What to Do

Read the story with your child and look at the picture together. Then have your child circle words in the story that end with **-each** and draw a line under words that end with **-ear**.

To Parents

This week your child learned to read and write words from the **-each** and **-ear** word families.

I go to my dad's every year. He lives near the beach. Dad said he would teach me to ride the waves. I had a fear of the big waves. But not anymore!

What to Do Next

Work together with your child to write a story using words from the **-each** and **-ear** word families.

Everyday Literacy: Reading and Writing • EMC 2419 • © Evan-Moor Corp.

A Skate Party

Word Families
-ake, -ate

Vocabulary
-ake: bake, cake, fake, flake, Jake, lake, make, quake, rake, shake, snake, take
-ate: date, gate, Kate, late, mate, plate, rate, skate, state

High-Frequency Words: a, can, for, is, it, like, on, please, put, she, take, the, them, there, this, to, what, we, your

Day 1

SKILLS:

Phonemic Awareness
• Generate sounds from letter patterns
• Blend two to four phonemes into recognizable words

Phonics/ Word Analysis
• Read words with common spelling patterns
• Read high-frequency and sight words
• Read regularly spelled one-syllable words

Comprehension
• Identify story characters
• Identify main idea
• Respond to who, what, where, how questions

Introducing Long *a* Word Families: *-ake, -ate*

Distribute the Day 1 activity page. Say: *This week we are reading and writing two long **a** word families: /āk/ and /āt/.*

• *Point to the **-ake** box at the top of the page. Say /āk/. (/āk/) Point to the first word. It has two vowels, **a** and **e**. The **a** makes a long sound: /ā/. The **e** does not make a sound; it is silent. Say the letter sounds with me: /k-ā-k/. Blend the sounds together: **cake**. Point to the next word: /j-ā-k/, **Jake**. Point to the last word: /b-ā-k/, **bake**. What word part is the same in all of these words? (/āk/) These words belong to the **-ake** word family.*

• *Now point to the **-ate** box. Say /āt/. (/āte/) Point to the first word. Say the letter sounds with me: /g-ā-t/, **gate**. Point to the next word: /s-k-ā-t/, **skate**. Point to the last word: /p-l-ā-t/, **plate**. What word part is the same in all of these words? (/āt/) These words belong to the **-ate** word family.*

Listening to the Story

Say: *Listen as I read you a story that has words from the **-ake** and the **-ate** word families. The title of this story is "A Skate Party."*

My friend Jake is having a birthday party on Friday. He can take three friends to Skate World. He invited me to come. Jake's mom is going to bake a cake. She will pick us up at the gate after school. We can skate and play roller tag. After that, we'll each have a plate of cake and ice cream. I'll remember to say, "Thanks for a great party, Jake!"

Thinking About the Story

Distribute pencils. Guide students in discussing the story. Say:

• *Who is having a birthday? (Jake) What word part do you hear at the end of **Jake** and **cake**? (/āk/) Which word family do those words belong to: **-ate** or **-ake**? (-ake) Make a dot on **Jake**.*

• *What was this story about? (a party at Skate World) What did the characters eat? (a plate of cake and ice cream) What word part do you hear at the end of **skate** and **plate**? (/āt/) Which word family do those words belong to? (-ate) Write an **X** on something the children **ate**.*

Day 1 picture

Listening for *-ake* and *-ate* Words

Guide a discussion that helps students recall yesterday's story. Say:

Our story was about Jake's birthday party.

- *Where did the children go? (Skate World) Which word family does the word **skate** belong to? (-ate)*

Then distribute pencils and the Day 2 activity. Say:

- *Point to the **-ake** word family at the top of the page. Let's read the **-ake** words together. Point to each word as we read: **lake, rake, flake**.*

- *Now point to the **-ate** word family at the top of the page. Let's read the **-ate** words together. Point to each word as we read: **gate, skate, plate**.*

- *Look at number 1. It shows a gate. What is the first sound in **gate**? (/g/) Which word part do you hear at the <u>end</u> of **gate**? (/āt/) Write the word **gate** in the boxes.*

Repeat the process for numbers 2 through 6. Then say:

- *Look at the words at the bottom of the page. Read each word. Circle the words that belong to the **-ake** word family. Underline the words that belong to the **-ate** word family. Let's read the first word together: **late**. Which word family does **late** belong to? (-ate) Draw a line under **late**.*

Repeat the process for the remaining words.

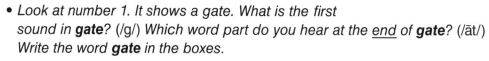

Day 2 activity

SKILLS:
Phonemic Awareness
- Generate sounds from letter patterns
- Segment onset and rime

Phonics/ Word Analysis
- Read words with common spelling patterns
- Read high-frequency and sight words
- Read regularly spelled one-syllable words

Comprehension
- Recall details
- Respond to who, what, where, how questions

Writing
- Print legibly and space letters and words appropriately

Writing *-ake* and *-ate* Sentences

Reread the Day 1 story. Then guide a discussion about the story by saying:

Our story was about Jake's birthday.

- *What did the children eat at the party? (cake and ice cream) Which word family does **cake** belong to? (-ake)*

Distribute pencils and the Day 3 activity. Say:

*We are going to read, trace, and then write sentences that have **-ake** and **-ate** words.*

- *Point to the first sentence. Move your finger under each word as we read together: **Bake a cake**. Which words are from the **-ake** word family? (bake, cake) Now trace the sentence, then write the sentence again on the line below. Put your pencil down when you are finished.*

- *Point to the next sentence. Let's read it together: **It is for Jake**. Which word is from the **-ake** word family? (Jake) Trace the sentence, then write the sentence again on the line below. Put your pencil down when you are finished.*

After students complete sentence 2, have them read sentences 1 and 2 aloud. Repeat the process for sentences 3 and 4.

Day 3 activity

SKILLS:
Phonics/ Word Analysis
- Read words with common spelling patterns
- Read high-frequency and sight words
- Read regularly spelled one-syllable words

Comprehension
- Recall details
- Respond to who, what, where, how questions

Writing
- Print legibly and space letters and words appropriately

Day 4

SKILLS:

Phonics/ Word Analysis

- Read words with common spelling patterns
- Read high-frequency and sight words

Comprehension

- Recall details
- Respond to who, what, where, how questions

Writing

- Print legibly and space letters and words appropriately

Reading *-ake* and *-ate* Words

Reread the Day 1 story if necessary. Then guide a discussion about the story by saying:

There was a boy in our story.

- *What was the boy's name?* (Jake)
- *What word family is that name from?* (-ake)
- *Where did he take his friends?* (Skate World)
- *What word family is **skate** from?* (-ate)

Distribute pencils and the Day 4 activity. Say:

Listen carefully and follow my directions.

- *Put your finger on the first sentence. Move your finger under each word as we read it together: **Please take this rake**. Underline the words from the **-ake** word family.* (take, rake) *Draw a line to the picture that matches the sentence.*

Repeat the process for numbers 2 through 4. Then point to the word box at the bottom of the page and say:

- *Point to this word box. Let's read the words together: **plate**, **cake**, **bake**. Each sentence below is missing one word. Look at the picture next to each sentence. Write one of the words from the word box to complete each sentence.*

Day 4 activity

Day 5

SKILLS:

Phonemic Awareness

- Recognize a new spoken word when a phoneme is added, changed, or removed

Phonics/ Word Analysis

- Read words with common spelling patterns

Oral Language Activity

Reinforce this week's word families by using a phoneme substitution activity. Introduce and model the call-and-response below.

All: *Let's make a word family; we'll have fun.*
All: *Let's make a word family; **-ake** is one.*

Students: *What's the word?*
Teacher: *The word is **lake**.*
Students: *What do we change?*
Teacher: *Change /l/ to /m/.*
Students: ***Make!***
Teacher: ***Make** is the word.*

Students: *What's the word?*
Teacher: *The word is **make**.*
Students: *What do we change?*
Teacher: *Change /m/ to /t/.*
Students: ***Take!***
Teacher: ***Take** is the word.*

Continue the chant using **bake**, **snake**, **cake**, **rake**, **quake**.

Then repeat the chant using -**ate** family words: /d/ date, /f/ fate, /g/ gate, /k/ Kate, /l/ late, /pl/ plate, /sk/ skate, etc.

Extension: Write -**ake** and -**ate** words on index cards. Recite the chant above using letter names instead of sounds. For example, say: *Change m to t*. After students say the new word, hold up the corresponding word card (**take**) as you say the word.

Home–School Connection p. 170
Spanish version available (see p. 2)

Name _____

A Skate Party

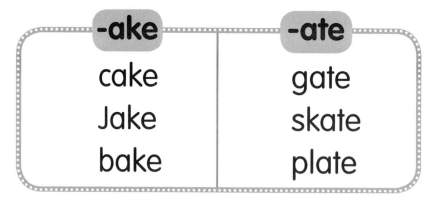

-ake	**-ate**
cake	gate
Jake	skate
bake	plate

Everyday Literacy: Reading and Writing • EMC 2419 • © Evan-Moor Corp.

Name _____

A Skate Party

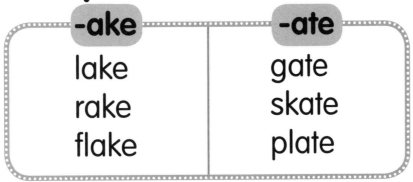

-ake	-ate
lake	gate
rake	skate
flake	plate

Write the correct word in the boxes.

1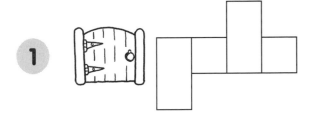

2

3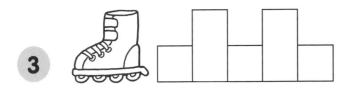

4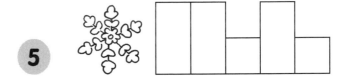

5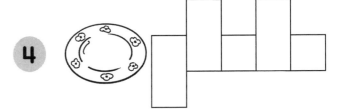

6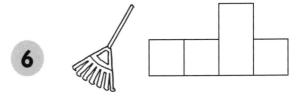

Circle the **-ake** words. Underline the **-ate** words.

(-ake) -ate

late	bake	make	date	rate	fake
cake	state	shake	mate	quake	Kate

Name _____

A Skate Party

Read the sentence. Trace the sentence. Then write the sentence on the line below.

1. Bake a cake.

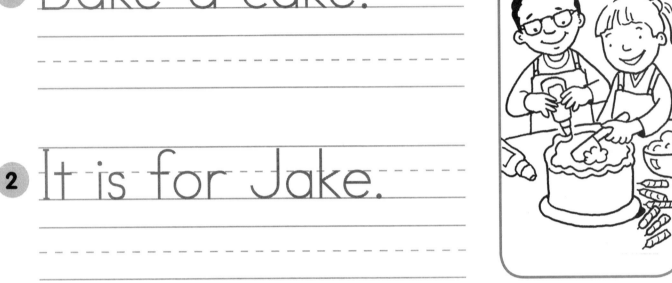

2. It is for Jake.

3. There is Kate.

4. She can skate.

Everyday Literacy: Reading and Writing • EMC 2419 • © Evan-Moor Corp.

A Skate Party

Read the sentence. Draw a line to the correct picture.

1 Please take this rake.

2 Please take this snake.

3 What is the date?

4 This is a skate.

Write the correct word to complete each sentence.

plate   cake   bake

1 We like _____.

2 She likes to _____.

3 Put them on a _____.

Name _____

A Skate Party

What to Do
Read the story with your child and look at the picture together.
Then have your child circle words in the story that end with **-ake**
and draw a line under words that end with **-ate**.

WEEK 20

**Home–School
Connection**

To Parents
This week your child
learned to read and write
words from the **-ake** and
-ate word families.

Jake has a birthday. His mom will bake a cake.
We can all go skate. We can have a plate of cake.
We won't be late. Happy Birthday, Jake!

What to Do Next
Work together with your child to write a story using words from the **-ake** and **-ate** word families.

Answer Key

Week 1   **Day 2**   **Day 3**   **Day 4**

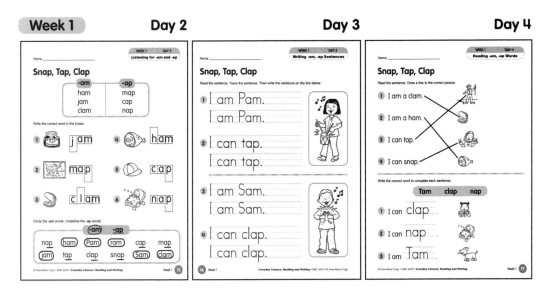

Week 2   **Day 2**   **Day 3**   **Day 4**

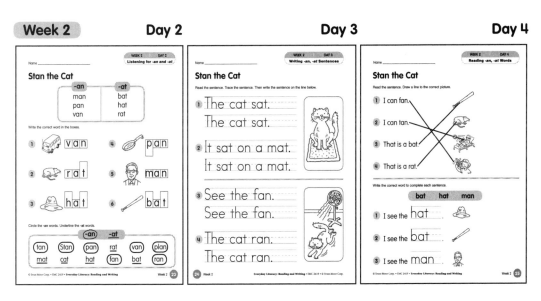

Week 3   **Day 1**   **Day 2**   **Day 3**   **Day 4**

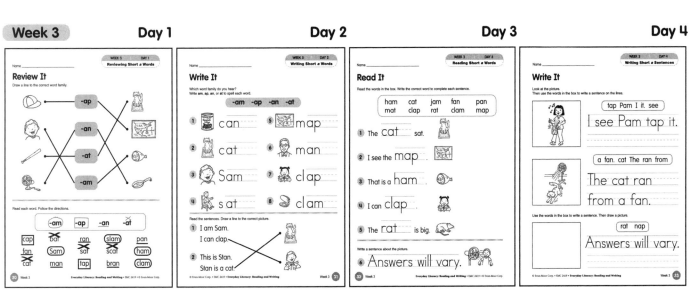

Week 4
Day 2
Day 3
Day 4

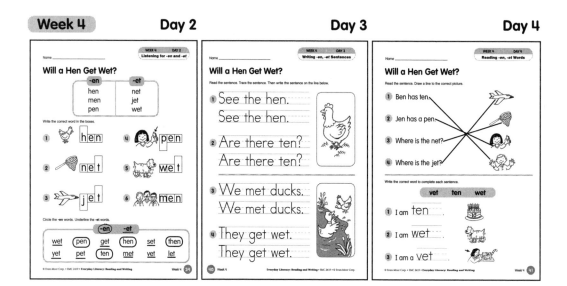

Week 5
Day 2
Day 3
Day 4

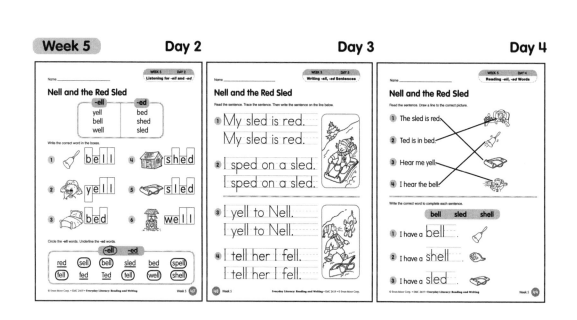

Week 6
Day 1
Day 2
Day 3
Day 4

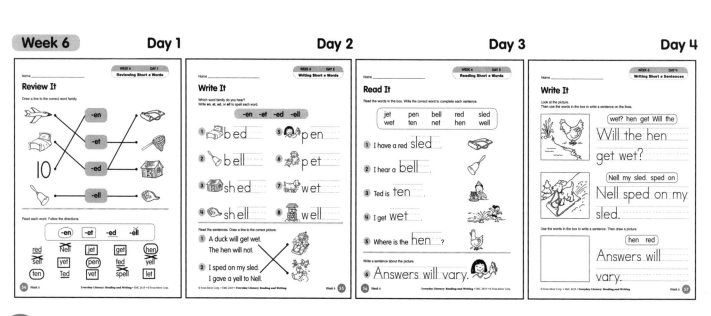

Week 7

Day 2 · **Day 3** · **Day 4**

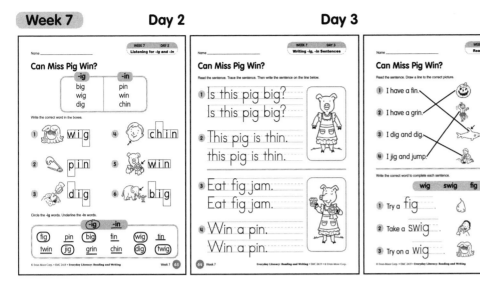

Week 8

Day 2 · **Day 3** · **Day 4**

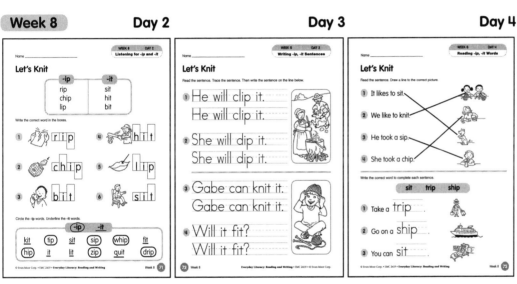

Week 9

Day 1 · **Day 2** · **Day 3** · **Day 4**

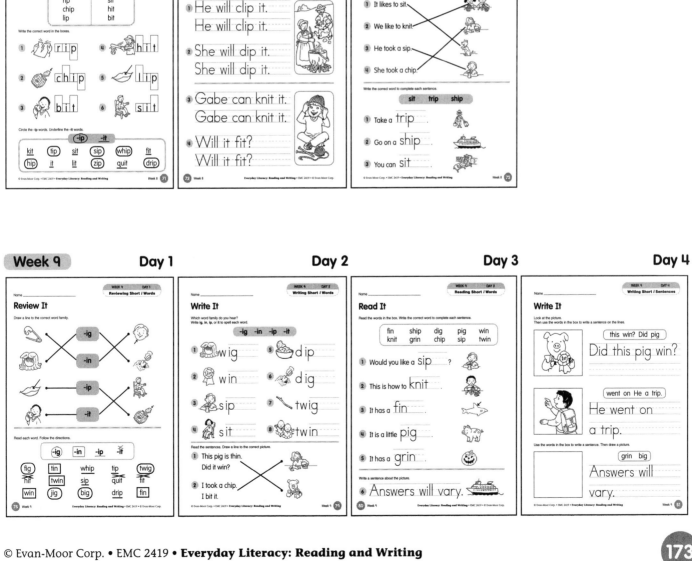

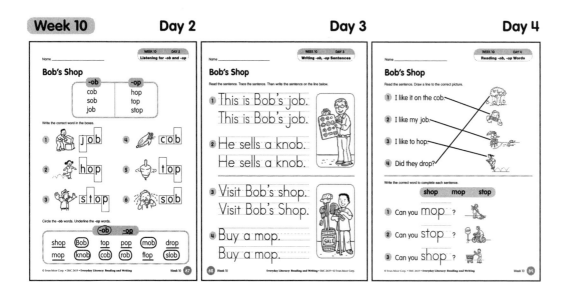

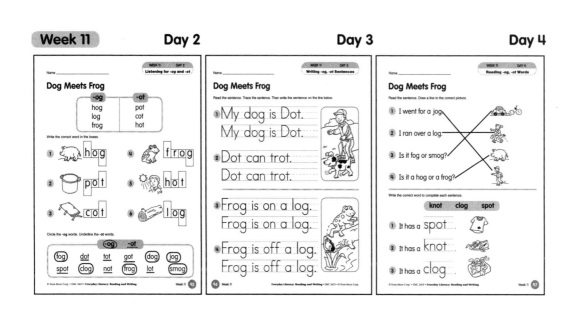

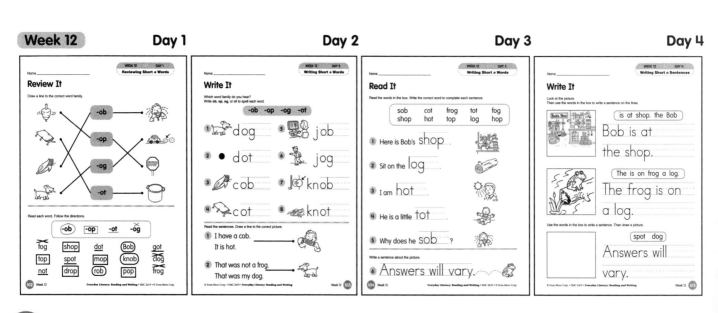

Everyday Literacy: Reading and Writing • EMC 2419 • © Evan-Moor Corp.

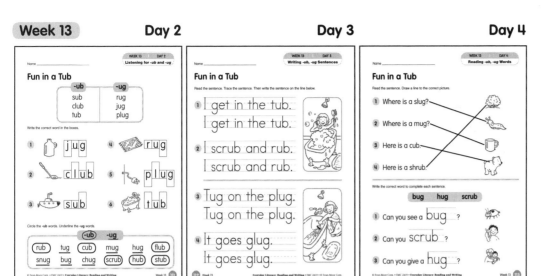

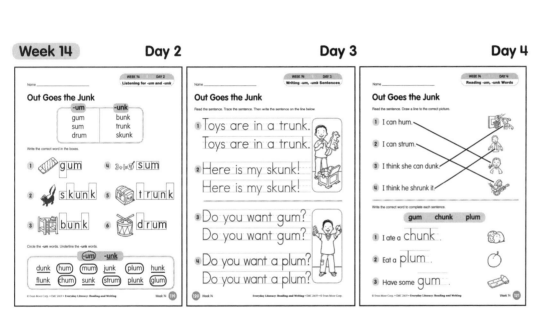

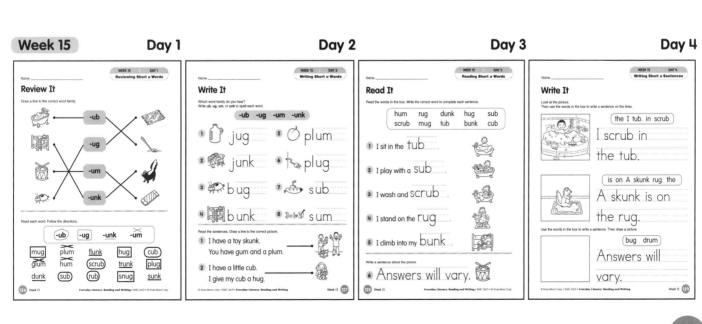

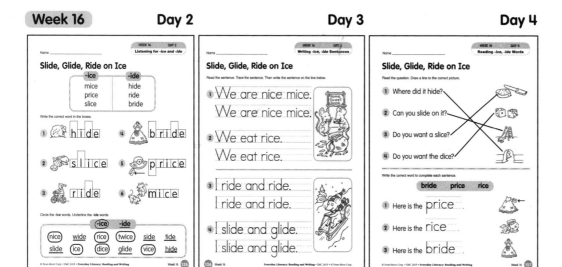

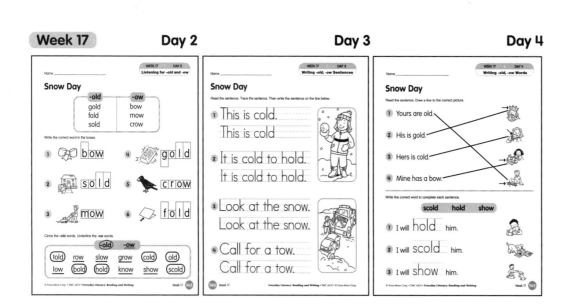

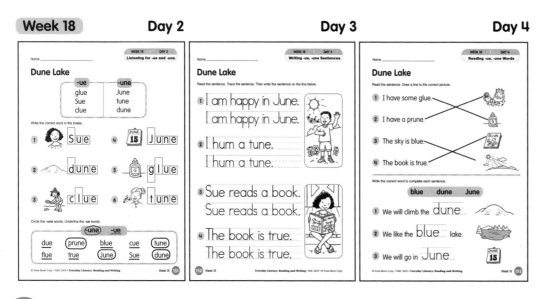